The Light of Wisdom

A Commentary on Selected Verses from
Sri Ramana Maharshi's
Supplement of the Forty Verses on Reality

and

Five Verses on the One Self
(Ekatma Panchakam)

by Nome

Published by
Society of Abidance in Truth (SAT)
1834 Ocean Street
Santa Cruz, CA 95060 USA
web: www.SATRamana.org
email: sat@satramana.org

Contents

Om Namo Bhagavate Sri Arunachala Ramanaya

California,
Campbell 12020 3 Nov

Introduction

This book consists of a commentary on selected verses of the *Supplement of the Forty Verses on Reality* and *Five Verses on the One Self, Ekatma Panchakam*. The English verses are as they appear in the 1974 fourth edition of *The Collected Works of Ramana Maharshi* published by Sri Ramanasramam.

Earlier, SAT published a commentary accompanying an English translation of *Saddarsanam,* which is the Sanskrit version of the *Forty Verses on Reality.* The commentary on *Saddarsanam,* entitled *An Inquiry Into the Revelation of Truth and Oneself* (as it appears in the SAT Publication, *Saddarsanam, and An Inquiry Into the Revelation of Truth and Oneself),* was derived from transcripts of spiritual instruction imparted at the SAT Temple. This present book is also derived from transcripts of the spiritual instruction expounded at the SAT Temple during retreats in 2011, 2012, 2013 and 2017. Questions raised in dialogues have been omitted here, and the answers have been edited to blend into a single essay. Verse numbers pertain to their placement in the *Supplement of the Forty Verses on Reality.* Only some of the verses have been selected and, hence, the title of this work. Of the verses selected, some were composed by Sri Ramana, and some were composed by other sages, such as Adi Sankaracarya and Vasishtha.

Acknowledgments

Deep appreciation and gratitude are here expressed to Sri Ramanasramam for permission to use these sacred verses, Carol Johnson and Grant Summerville for transcription of the SAT retreats presented in this book, Raman Muthukrishnan and Sangeeta Raman for proofreading and distribution of SAT publications, Raymond Teague for proofreading, Sasvati for design, layout, and seeing to the printing of this book, Sivakumar Chandran for the cover photo, Richard Schneider, Laura Pace and all the SAT Temple devotees whose support of the temple and the publication of these teachings of Self-Knowledge has made this book possible.

Supplement of the Forty Verses on Reality

Om Namo Bhagavate Sri Ramanaya
Om Sri Gurubhyo Namah

Reality is certain. It is certain of itself.

Upon Self-Realization, Sri Bhagavan remained, forever afterward, with absolute certainty. About what was this certainty? It is the Truth. What is the Truth? This certainty of the Knowledge of Reality involves the identity of the one who realizes and that which is realized, for that is the Self. If it were knowledge about something else, there would be scope for modification, but, as this is Self-realization, it is invariable and ever-existent.

What is the Self? Knowing this, you find peace that is changeless, happiness that is perfectly full, and freedom without the least trace of bondage or limitation. What is this Self that is to be found? Sri Bhagavan has very graciously given an abundance of spiritual instruction of utmost clarity so that everyone can realize. What is it that you are attempting to realize? It is not something else, but yourself. So, what is your Self?

Invocation

That in which this entire universe is established, to which it pertains, out of which it arises, for which it exists, by which it comes into being, and which it really is—that is the self-existent Reality, the Truth. Let us worship That in the heart.

That in which this entire universe is established. What is the existence in which everything, without exception, is established? The existence, the truth of which is sought through Self-inquiry, is not a small thing. Smallness is if there is misidentification with the body, but he says of this existence, **That in which this entire universe is established.** Existence is. Whether you regard the universe as something solidly real, as a play of energy, as a temporary dream, as a mere illu-

1

sion, or in any other way, in what is it established? There is Existence that is not confined to or defined by the forms of the universe but in which the universe is established, apart from which nothing is. That Existence is your existence. Abandon the narrow-mindedness of the misidentification with the body, and know your existence as **That in which this entire universe is established.** It is indivisible and illimitable.

Contemplate in what the entire universe, with all of its space, time, objects, and occurrences, is contained. **That in which this entire universe is established** is infinite, beyond the conception of "infinite." Whether it seems real or is known to be otherwise, in what is the universe established? There is immeasurable existence in which the entire universe rests. The Existence is self-existent. The universe depends on it, but it does not depend on the universe.

Where is the universe? If the misidentification with the body prevails, the universe appears as if external to oneself. If the misidentification with the body is relinquished, the universe is within you. Where else could it be?

To which it pertains means for whom it appears. Existence is the only substance everywhere, at all times, and it is your Existence, of the nature of Consciousness, for which all this is. You are not a body-bound individual but rather the infinite, eternal Existence in which the entire universe is established and for whom it pertains.

To which it pertains. If there is the universe, there is some purpose of all of it. To what does all this pertain? All of this that is manifested pertains to something that is un-manifested. This entire universe pertains to the vast, transcendent Existence in which it is established. Spread out in all of its magnificence, it is but a faint reflection of something incomparable, and that something is to be found within. That is to be known as your quintessential Existence. This quintessential Existence is self-existent, unlike all of the names and forms of the universe, which depend upon it. The self-existent is the Truth. That which has a dependent existence is not the truth. The Truth, real Being, is self-existent. That is your real identity. As an embodied being, you pertain to something unembodied and not individualized. When you worship that in the heart, you find that you are not an embodied, individual being at all but that which is worshiped. In the Realization of that are great bliss and final peace.

Do you have any experience of a universe, apart from the knowing of it? Thus, it is within you; in you, it is established, and by you, it is known.

Out of which it arises: You are that from which all this comes forth. It comes forth, or appears, only in you. Relinquish the limited conception of the body-bound ego, and recognize the Existence from which all this comes, for whom it all is, and in which all of it appears. As an individual, you are assumed to be just a small part, but your nature is Existence and not the mere individual, which is but an illusion. As a body, you are miniscule, and everything else is apart from, or outside, of you. Abandoning the misidentification with the body, find all of this as established in you and arising from you. You sleep, and nothing appears. You dream or wake, and everything appears. Where does it appear? That unformed Existence, from which all arise, in which all appear, and which remains changeless, immeasurably vast and formless, is you.

Out of which it arises. The universe has a source. The source is not to be found in the universe. The source is of a transcendent nature. Out of what great source does all of this appear? All of this does not arise of its own accord. The great Existence lends, as it were, a speck of itself so that all of this appears. The Existence is to be known as your essential Being. What we worship, what we are devoted to, and what we meditate upon and inquire into is not something that appears in this universe but rather that from which the universe arises. That, out of which the universe arises, shares none of the limitations of the forms that appear in the universe. The self-existent is illimitable. It is just this self-existent one, the Truth, that you really are.

Out of which it arises. What is the source of all this? The source of "this" cannot be found in "this." It is found in the nature of the "I."

For which it exists, by which it comes into being. For whom is this apparent existence? The universe does not declare its own existence. Who knows of the existence? The knowing one is the one Existence, and it is by the power of this Existence that anything else can seem to be. There could not even be the thought of the existence of all this without that Existence. In what does all this appear? By whom is it known? By what great power can something seem to exist? Indeed, the entire universe exists by a power that is universe-transcendent, pure Existence, and this Existence is truly you.

For which it exists. For whom is this universe? You suppose that it is. What is the nature of "you"? You cannot be defined by any of the forms that appear in the universe, whether such is a body or any other form. What is that for which it exists? That for which it exists is self-existent and does not exist for another. The universe exists for you. It depends on you, but you do not depend on any other. You are not a small, individualized, particularized, embodied being. You are the self-existent Reality, the Truth, and it is that which should be worshiped most inwardly.

By which it comes into being. The Self, the true Existence, is not only the substance out of which the universe is formed, but it is the power that so forms. It is that out of which all arise and by which all come into being. It is both the material and the instrumental, or efficient, causes. It is self-existent and immeasurable, though it is described as being the material and instrumental causes. A cause assumes that something has actually happened. It assumes some semblance of difference. The Reality, Existence, is without differences and, therefore, free of cause and effect.

For which it exists. Does the universe proclaim its own existence, or do you say to yourself, "It is; it exists"? From where does the sense of being real come? **By which it comes into being.** Such vast power has a source. Where is the source? If there is no experience of a universe as an external entity, but it is within you, and if it is utterly dependent on the knowledge of it, in order to even appear, it has no reality except from you, Thus, **which it really is.**

And which it really is. What is the nature of the entire universe? It is the very same nature as you. What is the nature of you? Just as you are not the bodily form, so the nature of all this is not the universe of forms, but, in illusion, some existence

4

is mistaken to be the form of all this. Setting yourself free of such delusion, know the existence as it is. The nature of the entire universe, the very nature from which it seems to spring forth, the very nature that seems to be the power that brings it forth, the very nature that knows it and to which it pertains, the very nature in which it is established, that Existence is the only thing that actually exists. It is the undefined, formless Existence that is the beginning, middle, and end of everything. This entire universe is only that self-existent, real Being perceived as such.

There is only this one absolute Existence. It alone is the substance, and it alone is the power. It alone is the knower, for its nature is pure Consciousness. There is nothing apart from that. This entire universe is nothing at all, except the one, undifferentiated, immeasurable, boundless Existence. Existence is to be worshiped in the heart and realized to be our true Self.

The nature of all this is the nature of the "I." What is the nature of "I"? The "I" truly is just Existence. All of this is just Existence, yet Existence, itself, has no form. Existence, which is Consciousness, is forever unmodified. When it is said, **"Which it really is,"** or, "All this is Brahman," the emphasis is on Brahman, the Existence, and not the form of this world, though the form, also, has no separate existence.

That is the self-existent Reality, the Truth. Let us worship That in the heart. The universe is dependent upon Existence. Everything that you think about depends on your own existence even to appear, but the existence, itself, which is the existence that seems to be you and that seems to be this universe, is self-existent and does not depend on anything else in order to be. The self-existent Reality, which alone is the Truth, is to be realized with certainty. Indeed, such realization of the self-existent Being of the Self alone can contain absolute certainty.

Let us worship That in the heart. Let us know, with a knowledge that is certainly divine, the infinite, eternal Existence as the very core of our Being, our actual Self. The heart is not a place, for all the places that can be are contained in the universe, and the universe is contained in the Existence, which is the heart. It cannot be defined in space or time. Timeless and

5

space-less is the self-existent Reality. That is the truth, that is the heart of you, and that is your actual Being. To know yourself as That and abide as That is true Knowledge.

Let us worship That in the heart. That which is in the innermost recess of one's being is to be meditated upon and known. It is that to which we pour forth our devotion. It is **the self-existent Reality, the Truth.** When one truly turns within, what one comes to know, experience and realize is not small. It is not limited to the confines of a person or the individual's mind. What is within is that in which the entire universe is established. As soon as the I-am-the-body misidentification is abandoned, the scope of that which is being realized becomes very clear.

Regard only that which is self-existent as the truth of you. Inquire within and discern that which is self-existent. That does not depend on the waking state of mind, a dreaming state of mind, or any other state. The self-existent does not depend on sense perception and does not depend on a body. It does not depend on life and does not depend on thinking. Only the utterly self-existent is your real Being and true Knowledge. By inquiry, disidentify from all that is not self-existent. Everything manifested has a dependent existence. The self-existent alone is eternal. The eternal is alone the Truth. The Truth is alone worthwhile to identify with. Such identification, or abidance, is true Knowledge. It is your real home.

That is the self-existent Reality, the Truth. Whatever is dependent is unreal. That which is real is self-existent; it has no cause, it has no support, and it does not rely upon anything else in order to exist or to be known. The self-existent, your Being, is the self-known, for it is your Consciousness. **Let us worship That in the heart.** Worshiping That, there is no room for misidentification with the body or as an ego-entity. Where does this supreme worship occur? It perpetually occurs in the Heart, in the quintessence of Being. The highest form of worship is abidance as That.

The appearance of the universe is for some basis or is based upon some substratum. The basis, or substratum, is self-existent. It does not exist for or by anything else, which cannot be said of the universe. The universe has the self-existent real Being of the Self as its basis, but that basis has no other basis. It is the finality, the bare Reality. This Existence is the Truth. Lift your vision beyond name and form, the conceived and the perceptible, to realize this.

Let us worship That in the heart. True worship is the identification of your quintessential Being with That, the infinite, eternal Existence. Therefore, your spiritual practice is aimed at something very vast and enduring. It is something much greater than the person and the personal attributes. It is something much greater than an individual's momentary experience. The Realization of the Self is most interior, but it is utterly impersonal. Impersonal, it is full of Bliss. Full of Bliss, it is Perfection. That is the Perfection, the Perfect Fullness; all this is the Perfect Fullness. The Perfect Fullness of this, universally, is only the Perfection of That. When the universe has arisen and after it has dissolved, all that remains is the Perfect Fullness, the absolute Existence. Infinite, timeless Existence should be realized as your very Self, now and always. Such Knowledge constitutes the highest form of worship.

Worship is truly that in which the ego dissolves. In what Bhagavan reveals, not a trace of the ego remains, and, in it, is found the highest worship. This verse reiterates what is declared in a verse in *Yoga Vasishtha*. The self-existent is the Reality. It depends on nothing else in order to be. It is to be realized by searching deep within. One who realizes it stands as That. Such a one is Sri Bhagavan. We could say that, when he speaks, God speaks. So, we ought to listen very carefully. When he is silent, and he is perpetually so, it is the silence of the Absolute. We should listen to that very carefully, too.

By this verse, it is made abundantly clear that what you strive to realize by inquiry to know the Self is something infinite and eternal. It is not merely something personal, though it does lie at the center of everyone.

Of what significance are your thoughts in this universe? They do not amount to much contrasted with the rest of the universe, do they? The entirety of the universe is but a mere appearance in Brahman, while the actual truth of Brahman remains transcendent even of this. So, how important are your thoughts? Dedicate the life to the eternal, the infinite, and realize it as your true Self. Do not give your life to thoughts. Whether you think they exist or do not exist, how important are your thoughts, your particular individual experiences, etc., in the scope of the entire universe or as much of the universe as you can conceive? That which is to be known as the Self is no small personal thing but is that in which, by which, and for which the universe appears. If you wish to grasp the understanding that, in truth, thought actually does not exist, you must first relinquish all importance attributed to it and cease to regard what you think as being the truth.

The one Self alone exists, eternally. If a universe arises, it can arise only from That and in That, the infinite, the boundless and timeless. By what power could it arise? It could be only that of the very same Existence. For whom would it pertain? This is the very same Existence. This immeasurably vast, timeless Existence, the Absolute, is your true nature. You are not a speck within it. Rather, by his Knowledge and Grace, realizing that the individual is not such at all, you find one partless, indivisible Existence. This alone is your identity, the uncreated and the imperishable. To **worship That in the heart** is to meditate upon one's spiritual identity with That.

Verse 1

By association with the sages, attachment (to material things) is removed. When this is removed, the attachment of the mind also vanishes. Those who have got rid of their attachment of mind become one with That, which is motionless. They become liberated even while alive. Seek their company.

Where is attachment? Attachment is not in the Self, which is pure Bliss and Being, the taintless Consciousness. Where is attachment? Attachment is not in material things, for they are inert. Attachment is not in the body. Attachment appears only in the mind, and it is but a confusion regarding the nature and the source of happiness. One who pursues the truth to find the source of bliss loses attachment of all kinds. First is destroyed the attachment to worldly things by knowing the source of happiness. Then are destroyed all the other conceptions of the mind, which are confusion regarding the nature of one's own Being-Consciousness. If attachment, or confusion, is done away with, something remains that is of the nature of Existence and Bliss. It is motionless. It does not go out of itself, and it does not change. Its changelessness is its fullness. If it does not go out of itself, what, then, goes out? Illusion goes out into illusion. Understanding in this manner, externalization becomes impossible. You abide as the blissful, one infinite Existence, for which there is no outside and which does not become other than itself. This is truly being still, or motionless.

By association with the sages, attachment is removed. When this is removed the attachment of the mind also vanishes. Those who have got rid of their attachment of mind become one with That which is motionless. They are absorbed in the depths of blissful Being. Such a one has lost his individuality, and, therefore, we can only loosely speak of "such a one" or "the sages." They exist as solitary, indivisible Being-Consciousness-Bliss alone. Where there is not the least trace of individuality, there is no movement ever. There is just space-like, infinite, eternal Reality.

They become liberated even while alive. Freedom from the illusion of the body and the world is to be attained even while alive. When Knowledge dawns, ignorance is destroyed, because it is merely ignorance. Ignorance alone is the confusion constituting attachment. To be free of such is the right state. **Seek their company.** What happens in the company of the holy and the liberated? What actually is satsang? It is not a mere gathering of bodies. It is not just talking or some other activity. With what do you actually keep company? In satsang with Sri Bhagavan, with whom are we? What actually occurs? That it utterly transforms one's experience is doubtless, but what actually happens? In light, darkness cannot remain. The value of this can be known only by experience.

It is confusion that is referred to as attachment. Oneness, devotion, divine love, and certain Knowledge cannot be classified as attachment. Whether you feel he is always within you or you are always within him, or both and the distinctions dissolve, such cannot be regarded as attachment. Consider what actually occurs in keeping the company of the realized. It is obviously not a bodily sensation, activity, or bodily transformation that happens, and, with the dissolution of the individual, the supposed boundaries and divisions disappear. It transcends the body, so it has no boundaries of time and space. Even the assumed divisions of life and death do not apply. We keep his company even now.

The mind going outward is constituted merely of the confusion that is attachment. It is the connection of the reality and happiness of the Self with an idea of something. Without such attachment, you abide as the Self. That Self does not move at any time. It is absolutely motionless. In this Consciousness, no mind and world are actually ever created. The one who realizes the unchanging Reality is the Reality, for there is only one indivisible Existence. As the one to experience the external attachment does not exist, neither do his attachments or his confusions. The company of those who have realized this even in life reminds us of this irrefutable truth. If one traces the source of their words, he understands their meaning: Brahman, only Brahman.

That which is inert does not know itself. Something else knows it. If you trace this knowing to its essence, its source, you find that it is only one, and all of the divisions are inert illusions. Consciousness is indivisible and one without a second. Abiding in That, you see that there is only Consciousness everywhere and that there is no such thing as the inert.

Attachment consists of confusing the Self with what is not the Self, happiness with something that is not your happiness, reality with something that is actually entirely unreal, and Consciousness with something that is inert and does not know. If you trace the reality, the identity, and the happiness to their one source, attachment vanishes because the confusion vanishes. Then, you find that that which you previously regarded as the source alone exists, infinite and timeless.

In his commentaries, Sri Sankara proclaims the power of the words of the wise is actually the power of Brahman. The same holds true of their silence. When you listen and truly comprehend, you understand the meaning of what is said, which transcends all of the words and ideas, and real Knowledge dawns.

Keeping the company of the liberated destroys attachment, and you find that which is motionless. That is perfect.

By association with the sages, attachment is removed. The confusion regarding the nature and source of happiness is removed. The association is not bound to the confines of the body. Even today, we have the association of Sri Ramana. To associate is to feel the grace and to pour oneself into the spiritual instruction received. Egotism dissolves. Attachment is obliterated. Experiencing that, who would care for anything else? Being with that, what else would actually matter? It would be ridiculous if your mind were to confine him to a particular body, a particular place, or a particular time. Indeed, whenever you turn within, you have his association. It is by his association that you are able to turn within.

When attachment to material things is removed, the peace and bliss that are natural for you shine forth. When attachment to the entire world is removed, **the attachment of the mind also vanishes.** Attachment does not lie in physical things. Attachment is only the delusion of the mind. Attachment does not lie in the body or in the senses. It is the mind's way of thinking about these that **forms** the attachments.

If the attachments to objective things are relinquished, by virtue of such wise association and the inquiry implicit in such, the attachment to the mind, and the very belief that there is a mind, also is dissolved. **Those who have got rid of their attachment to mind, become one with That which is motionless.** If your mind is not attached to anything, what remains of your mind? If your mind would be nonattached to its own ideas, what would be left of your mind? It would be ridiculous to think that you would lose the attachment to your ideas if you were to still remain attached to things in the world. First you lose attachment to things in the world, by clarifying the understanding regarding happiness, and then you lose attachment to the mind, by ceasing to regard what you think as real.

With the questions of happiness and reality resolved, the question of identity also is resolved. What was previously considered to be your mind, or you, becomes one with that which is motionless. If there is no mistaken impression regarding the world, and you no longer adhere to any idea conjured in the mind, you remain as the motionless Consciousness, the pure Existence. You become one with That. Then, there is no more confusion regarding happiness, reality, or identity.

What brings this clarity? Association with the sages. They guide, they illumine, and they are proof of the Reality. They are the Light and are the Reality. If you lose your attachment of the mind and become one with that which is motionless, in the unswerving abidance as the eternal Self, you become liberated even while alive. Even while the body still appears, you are entirely bodiless. Even while the senses are active, you are completely detached from them and sense-transcendent. Even when thinking appears, you still remain the thought-free One. Identified with that which is motionless, the self-existent absolute Reality, you are liberated. You become Liberation, itself.

For such a one, there are no more distinctions as life and death. Just one self-existent, real Being perpetually is. If this is the aim, what should be done? **Seek their company.** If you have found such, do not relinquish such or be negligent concerning such. Such a sage is really your true Self. He appears to wake you up from the dream of being an ego, of being an embodied being. His purpose is the highest good.

In the vision of the wise, Being is Bliss. If happiness is known as one's own Self, one's own Being, there is no longer attachment to anything in this world. With the nonattached, unchanging peace of such should the seeker associate and merge.

Just one Existence is, and there is nothing with which or to which to become attached. The understanding about the nature and source of happiness, the happiness which the wise are, yields nonattachment to all things. When this attachment is removed, **the attachment of the mind,** which is the association of oneself with any concept whatsoever, **also vanishes.** Not attached to things, not attached to thoughts, not regarding the world as existent, and not regarding the mind as existent, what happens for one? **Those who have got rid of their attachment of mind become one with That, which is motionless.** By nonattachment, one becomes inward-turned. Turning inward, one passes beyond the belief in an existent mind. Passing beyond the mind, one remains simply as That, the absolute Existence, which has no motion. It does not change, does not go in, does not go out, and does not go anywhere, but simply just is as it is, always. That is Brahman. That is the Truth. That is the Self, and That is what you are. Those who have realized That are That. To have association, or satsang, with Sri Bhagavan is to be with Truth. It may appear to be association with one who knows the Truth, but, in the Knowledge of Truth, Being is identical with knowing. One's identity is completely consumed, and there remains not the least trace of the false belief in individuality. So, to associate with him is to associate with Brahman. **They become liberated even while alive.** Such sages abide in the bodiless, individuality-less state. Appearing as a sage, he is really, completely the absolute Supreme Brahman. **Seek their company,** because it is the root and the fruit of the highest good.

There must be some understanding, some intuition, even if ever so vague, that happiness is to be found within so that one would seek the company of sages. Without this, such sages would be of very little interest to one. Happiness is within, and the knowledge that it is within is the essence and substance of nonattachment. What else is attachment but confusion regarding the nature and source of happiness? Implicit in attachment is confusion regarding the eternal and the non-eternal, for one wants happiness to last. One does not want suffering and what is transitory. By the company and instruction of sages, the intuition about the source and nature of happiness is further clarified and strengthened.

The same power that dissolves attachment to outer things also dissolves the various attachments or tendencies in the mind. Just as happiness is not found in external things but is found within, likewise, such happiness is not found in mental concepts and mental tendencies but is found within. That which urges detachment prompts disidentification, as well.

If you eliminate the attachments of the mind, which are the mind's clinging to its own ideas, one becomes **That, which is motionless.** To be motionless means to remain in the Self, as the Self, the changeless abidance as the changeless.

If you abide as the Self, which is Self-Knowledge, **you become liberated even while alive.** Even while alive, there is no further misidentification with the body. Even while alive, the false notion of a separate individuality is dissolved. Become liberated. It is freedom from all of the imagined bondage. Bondage has no existence apart from the one who believes in it. So, what do you believe yourself to be and what are you truly? Do they coincide?

Seek their company. Such company is not only external. What if Bhagavan were with you all of the time? He is. Seek that company.

Verse 6

"Who is God?" "He who knows the mind." "My mind is known by me, who am spirit." "Therefore, you are God and also because scripture declares, 'God is one.'"

Something all-seeing observes your mind. No matter what the state of mind may be and no matter what form the mind may seem to take, something knows it and is unaffected by it. What is that? It is beyond any limitation and any condition imagined by the mind, for all of that is merely the known. That which knows the mind, untouched by the mind, is truly spiritual. Spirit transcendent of every concept of the mind is God.

God is one. If you think that you are distinct from God, God is two. There is God who is God, and there is you, who are God. To have faith that God is one means that there can be no separate individual and no separate universe, because, if they were separate or distinctly existing in any way whatsoever, they would be gods; but **God is one.** For one who has the Knowledge of God, there is no scope for duality and no possibility of multiplicity.

What sees the mind is not small. The individual may be regarded as an illusory play of the mind. What sees the mind is not the individual. What is not an individual possesses none of the characteristics of an individual. In the view, "I see my mind," what is the nature of the "I"? It cannot possibly correspond to anything that appears in the mind because it is the seer thereof. Since the entire world is only within the mind, if you want to know God, you must discern within yourself that which is behind, or beyond, the mind. That which is transcendent over the world and the mind can be only God. If you really have faith in God, God alone is.

Regarding seeing God without Self-Knowledge, in another text, Sri Bhagavan states that such is only a mental image. Fortunately, God does not have the same mental image. Who has the mental image? God is certainly far, far superior to and above the so-called "me," but is there a "me"?

If there is the idea of existing as a separate individual, a jiva, God will seem to be something else. The fact that this duality is illusory is brought out time and again in the *Ribhu Gita*. Adi Sankara declares that if one knows the real nature of Iswara, the Lord, he finds only Brahman, and, if one knows the real nature of jiva, the individual, he finds only Atman, the Self. He and other sages and numerous scriptures declare that Atman and Brahman, the Self and the Absolute, are identical; they are one and the same thing. So, the disciples of these sages were taught Tat tvam asi, That you are. If you retain the idea of being an individual, a "me," and attempt to know God, the most that you will attain is a concept in relation to the "me." That is not God. That which sees the play of the mind, untouched by it, is God. Since the existence of God is completely one with no parts possible, there is no room left for this "me." The singular "I" that is not touched by any of the divisions in the mind is God. To think of oneself as distinct from God, even by a particle, is egotistical.

Who knows the mind? The mind does not know itself. Something illumines, or knows, the mind. He who knows the mind cannot possibly be known by the mind. The one who knows is necessarily beyond every mental conception. Within the mind, multiplicity appears. Beyond the mind, how could multiplicity be possible?

My mind is known by me, who am spirit. Therefore, you are God. All the multiplicity or division appears only in the mind. Beyond the mind, such is impossible. If I know the mind, I cannot be anything contained in the mind. Therefore, not a single thought applies to me. The inconceivable one is God. God is what you are. An idea within the mind cannot be God. God transcends that. Beyond the mind, in that in which there is no thought, how could there be any division between God and oneself? Any such distinction or separation is only in the mind, just an idea about God, an idea about oneself.

Beyond the ideas, beyond the mind, lies the solitary, indivisible Consciousness, the one knower of all minds, unknown by any mind. The knower of the mind is not individualized. To think of the knower as individualized is to think of the knower of the mind in terms of being in the mind. It is to apply an idea to that which is beyond all ideas. Abandoning such a tendency to misidentify, what remains of the knower? What is it that knows your mind?

Scripture declares, "God is one." If God is one, that leaves no scope for another, such as yourself or a world or anything else. If you think such other things actually exist, such is polytheism. If God is truly one, as the scriptures declare, God is the solitary Existence, and there is no other kind of existence to you or to anything else. God is one. All else is just a product of the mind appearing in the mind. The mind, too, does not have a separate existence, but rests upon the knower of it. Who is he who knows the mind? Who is God? If only the false differences imagined in the mind are abandoned, all this will be comprehended. Cease to regard yourself in terms of what is conceived in thought, and all this will be perfectly clear.

There is one who knows the mind. That one is God. Quite obviously, you cannot hide something in the mind from God. God is omniscient, all-seeing. You see everything of the mind; nothing in the mind is hidden from you. Nothing of the truth is hidden, and nothing of delusion is hidden. The Knower of the mind can only be one. Multiplicity is possible only in the known, the objective. In the nonobjective, there is no form by which to delineate the multiplicity. A plurality of knowers, a multiplicity of consciousnesses, is not possible. The Consciousness, which is absolutely One, that knows the mind, but which the mind cannot know, is God. Inquire to know your nature as God, and do not mistake yourself to be anything that is the content of the mind.

Indeed, **who is God?** The attempt to understand God without knowing yourself is just to engage in the formation of a mental concept. God is transcendent of such. So, who is God?

Inconceivable, God is the knower of the mind. What is it that knows all minds? Regard that which knows the mind, but is always unknown to the mind, alone as God, alone as spirit. Transcendent of the mind, interior to the mind, multiplicity or division is impossible. Only within the mind's imagination, or conception, is multiplicity apparent. Beyond thought, how could there be anything multiple? Beyond thought is the boundless, the formless. There cannot be two things that are formless. There cannot be two things that are boundless.

There is only One. That One you are. There is not a second to God. **Scripture declares, "God is One."** It does not mean that God is one object, and you are separate from it. It means God alone exists, and that Existence is your existence, apart from which you do not have another existence. To know God, by God's Knowledge of God, know yourself. To know yourself, inquire, "Who am I?" and discern the nonexistence of the individuality. All that is said here regarding the universe and God is self-evident to one who knows himself.

Verse 7

This verse is found in two works composed by Adi Sankara, *Eka-sloki* and *Sata-sloki*. These derive from a passage in the Upanishads.

"What provides you with light?" "By day, the sun, by night, a lamp." "What is the light that sees these lights?" "The eye." "What is the light that illumines the eye?" "The intellect." "What is it that knows the intellect?" "It is the 'I.'" "Therefore, you are the light of lights." When the teacher said this, [the disciple said,] "Truly, I am That."

If you trace the knowing inward, you arrive at the conclusive realization of yourself being pure Consciousness. What knows the world? **What provides you with light? By day the sun, by night a lamp; what is this light that sees these lights? The eye.** The experience of the universe is contained entirely within the sensations of it. The world, or universe, does not know itself. Something illumines it, knows it, through the senses. Apart from those sensations, the objective portion has no existence whatsoever and is certainly not self-known.

Asked, **"What is the light that illumines the eye?"** the eye and other senses, the answer is, **"the intellect."** Something shines in and through the mind and knows all the sensations, which in turn compose the entire sphere of objective experience. Apart from the mind, there is no experience and knowledge of the senses and the world. The senses do not know themselves. Something else knows them. It appears as the mind. What knows the mind? By what light is the mind seen? That alone can be "I," for the mind contains all that is objective. That which knows the mind, by whose light the mind is seen, must necessarily be nonobjective. The mind does not know itself. The "I" knows it. Here, the inquiry reaches its conclusion, for the "I" is self-known. The things, the senses, and the mind are not self-known. They depend on another to illuminate them. The "I," that which knows even the mind, is self-known and does not depend on anything else in order to be known. It does not depend on another source of illumination.

The "I" is only one. There are not two "I"s in you. There is just one "I," self-existent and self-known. It is the light of the world that is beyond the world, the light of the senses ungrasped by the senses, and the light of the mind not conceived by the mind. It is Brahman, which no sense and no thought can grasp. This is your real place. This is your true identity. You are, therefore, the light of all lights, the single light that alone shines through all that it transcends.

That which is truly "I," your identity, your existence, lies quite beyond the domain of words and thoughts. What is it that lies beyond words and thoughts? By whose light are the thoughts, the words, and all else known? The answer to the question is found not by guesswork or forming an idea but by complete absorption of your sense of identity in the light of Consciousness. The answer is of the nature of direct experience. The answer is of the nature of your very Being. Your abidance as That, the full absorption of your identity in That, is the nature of the answer to the inquiry.

Consciousness is not an attribute, just as Existence is not an attribute. An attribute is a quality that belongs to something else or a power or an ability that belongs to something else. Consciousness does not belong to anything else. At no time does Consciousness cease, just as at no time does Existence cease to exist. Consciousness neither does anything nor does anything do something to it.

Observe how the entire experience of the world is illumined by, or known by, your senses. Without the sensations, there would be no experience of a world. The light of the world, inclusive of all that are bright, like the sun and the moon, is the senses. What illumines, or knows, your senses? Your mind knows the senses. If it were not for the mind's knowledge, or illumination, there would be no experience of sensations. Trace the knowing further inward. What illumines the intellect? What is the light for your mind? The mind consists of innumerable thoughts of various permutations arranged in various modes and states. What illumines them? The mind does not know itself. What knows it? If it were not for this shining knowledge, there would be no experience of a mind.

Trace the knowing further inward. Beyond the mind, distinctions cease. You are left with your own Being. Your own Being is the all-illuminating Consciousness. What illumines Consciousness? Nothing else does. Nothing else knows it. It knows itself, by itself. It is not an object of perception or conception, but it is the light for all percepts and all concepts always. To know yourself to be that light is true Knowledge. Be free of mistaking yourself to be some illumined object. You are the illumination. If you misidentify as an object, from the mind to the forms of the world, the darkness of ignorance appears. If you know yourself to be the light of all lights, there is not a trace of darkness.

Distinguish what is objective and what is the Light. Though referred to as "light," it is not something to be seen with the eyes or visualized by the mind. By "light" is meant pure Knowledge; not percepts and concepts, but Knowledge.

The guru instructs in the manner of inquiry, what provides you with light, causing the Consciousness to become awake to itself and free from the darkness of delusion. It is the sadguru who informs the disciple, in the deepest possible way, that the disciple is truly the Light of lights. He reveals one's very identity, one's very Existence, the nature of Consciousness. By inquiring accordingly, following the instruction precisely, the state of "I-am-That," identity with Brahman, is realized.

It is a unique recognition, in that it is not constituted of ideas. It is not like recalling something from memory, though it is recalling something you always knew. It is the revelation of the ever-revealed.

The first step in diving deeper is the recognition of the need to proceed deeper. Thoroughness comes by questioning more. Thoroughness also comes by attempting to lift one's experience to the height indicated by the sages and the scriptures, rather than shrinking the meaning to fit into one's present perspective. Toward the spiritual instruction, the attitude should be, "What does this really mean? If this is so, what are the consequences?" If you have a strong conviction in the spiritual teaching bestowed by Sri Bhagavan, it is very worthwhile to compare and contrast your experience with it. If there is a difference, start questioning, "Why? What makes the difference?" The differences will be found to be due to various vasanas in the mind, various misidentifications and attachments. Such misidentifications and attachments are destroyed by questioning and examining them in the light of Self-inquiry and by association with sages. An attitude of eagerness will open the depth for you. One's own orientation, or approach, matters significantly. It is not necessary to attempt to train the mind to be able to imitate the explanations from various perspectives given in the spiritual instruction. What is necessary is to be thorough in applying such instruction, heard or read, to one's own experience.

By "light" is indicated knowing. What is it that truly knows? In relation to the objects, the senses seem to be the knower, but the senses themselves are the objects for the mind, for which the mind seems to be the knower. Who knows the mind? It is the "I." What, then, is the nature of "I"? What is the source of all knowing within you? That which is the source is self-luminous, self-knowing, and does not depend on any other instrument or source in order to know. You cannot be the known; you can be only the knower. All of the known is contained in the knowing and all of the knowing in the knower. To define the knower in terms of the forms of the known is a mistake. To realize the knower as the knower alone is the revelation of pure Consciousness. Your identity truly is only pure Consciousness, referred to as "the knower" in relation to all that is known. Just by itself, it transcends all definition.

In the discovery of Consciousness in meditation, what is the nature of the discoverer? The discrimination is not between two objective things, but rather the discernment of that which is nonobjective. The result is that Being is itself the Knowledge. The Knowledge, which can never be extinguished, which is its own source, and which is infinite and eternal, is here referred to as **light.**

Self-inquiry is non-conceptual, nonobjective Knowledge. It is not an activity; it is not a doing. Activities, of whatever kind, can yield only transient results. True Knowledge is of an eternal nature. Liberation is of an eternal nature. So, it is emphasized that action does not lead to Liberation. Self-Knowledge alone is Liberation. The complete dis-identification from all that is objective and the utter dissolution of an identity as an individual being are the inquiry and the Knowledge.

What is the nature of that which is aware of the object? What is the knower without an object to know?

The assumption of the objective, as something existing, occurs to whom? One Consciousness is all-illuminating. It is the light in all knowledge of whatever kind. When you think that you know something, you are actually knowing only the Self as that thing. The nature of the knowing is only the Self, also, and so it is for the knower, as well. One Self, in illusion, appears as three, the knower, the knowing, and the known. Upon inquiry into the knower, the individuality, being unreal, vanishes and, along with it, the objectifying outlook that supposes, "I know an object," or, "I have known objects in the past," etc. What has actually occurred? Just the Existence of the Self, which is the self-luminous Consciousness, is.

What is the light for you? What is the knower? Is your mind a knower? Someone knows the mind. The mind cannot be the knower. Beyond the mind, within you, what is there? Beyond the mind, there are no objects. Beyond the mind, there are not two. There is no multiplicity beyond the mind. Therefore, the verse concludes not with, "There is the light," but, "I am That." One's own Being is the Knowledge.

Direct experience, not ideas, is desirable.

We see objects; by what light do we see objects? Of course, there is physical light, but what is spoken of as light in the spiritual sense is knowledge. By your senses, you perceive all phenomena. So much so is this the case that we can say sensations compose the phenomena, and, apart from them, you have never experienced an object. The objects, therefore, are only sensations. The senses appear to know the objects; the objects do not know the senses. The senses do not know themselves. They are not self-effulgent. Something else knows them. Your mind knows your senses. So, the entire world is in the senses, and the entirety of the sensations is in your mind. Your mind knows the senses and their objects; the senses and their objects do not know your mind. The mind is not self-effulgent either; something else knows the mind. Beyond the mind, there is no name and form. Beyond the mind is only pure Consciousness, and that is your identity. You are not of the world, the body, the senses, or the mind. That which ought to be known as "I" is only this self-luminous Consciousness, the Light of lights. When the disciple truly understands the Reality, as taught by the guru, he realizes, and what he realizes is summed up in the phrase, **"Truly, I am That."** So, if we speak of Self-Realization as a state, it is a state of identity.

With all of the thinking that has ever been performed, you have not thought of your Self. You may have thought the word "Self," but you have not thought of your Self. If spiritual thought does not touch you, how much less does worldly thought touch you? There is One who understands you, and that One is God. Seek inwardly for the Light of all lights. You are not the mind; your nature is pure Consciousness. If you seek the Light of lights within yourself, it will turn out that there is not a thing to be called "the mind."

How do you see the world? By what light? If you see it by your senses, by what do you know the senses? You know the senses by your mind. Indeed, the senses are nothing more than a faculty within the mind itself. There is nothing external. What sees the mind?

The scriptures speak about the mind only to rid the aspirant of the false belief in it. The scriptures speak of objects, but do not do so with the intention of reinforcing the dualistic concept that objects exist. Rather, they speak of such only in the course of revealing the absolute Existence, which is God or Brahman. Likewise is it in the case of the mind, senses, the jiva, etc. Multiplicity is only possible with the senses and the mind. If the Light of which they speak is sense-transcendent and mind-transcendent, it can be only One. Since it is self-knowing, self-luminous, pure Knowledge, therefore the disciple said, **"Truly, I am That."** If there is anything, all of it is entirely within That. If there is not anything, That alone is. If you are That, you are the motionless. The Existence is only One.

Verse 8

In the interior of the heart-cavern, the one Brahman shines alone as "I-I," as the Self (Atman). Resort to the heart by diving deep within, through Self-inquiry or by subduing the mind along with the breath. You will thus become established in the heart.

In the interior space, which is not a physical space, but the space of your very Being, **the one Brahman shines.** It shines as "I-I," self-known, self-existent, and with no misconception about itself. This is to be realized. **Resort to the heart** means dive deep into it, find your refuge there, find sanctuary there, find peace there, find your freedom there, and find all of your happiness there **by diving deep within.** What is the nature of this diving? It is the return of the sense of identity and reality to their rightful place, which is the cave of the heart, the space of Being, which is Brahman. You do so by Self-inquiry and **subduing the mind along with the breath.** By "breath" is indicated prana. How do you subdue mind and prana? It is by ceasing to misidentify with such. How do you subdue them? By directing such wisely, and wisdom has its root in clarity of identity, which is knowledge of yourself. What you thus realize is ever-existent. **You will thus become established in the heart.** You find where you really are. Where are you really? Not in the world, not in the body, not in the prana, and not in the mind. Perhaps, you may be accustomed to thinking the center of all this is a small dot, but, in the spiritual quest, the closer you are to the center, the vaster it is. The universe is a dimensionless dot, and the vastness is of Brahman. "Brahman" indicates expansiveness.

Transcend the prana, which is in charge of all life activities, and transcend the mind. Inquire "Who am I?" Once you are established in the heart, there is no deviation from it. Once you know yourself as That, there is no motion ever. Once Self-Knowledge shines, ignorance is impossible. Once you are established in the heart, you cannot move, just as Brahman never becomes other than what it is.

What lies in your very center, figuratively referred to as **the "heart-cavern,"** the cave of the essence of your Being, the space that is at the center? Brahman, the vast Absolute. That shines as "I," in a state of identity of I-am-I, just the Self. Brahman is the Self. There is no other kind of self in existence. In this lies immortal bliss and perfect peace. How is it to be realized? **Resort to the heart by diving deep within.** Dive deep within so that you abide as your within-ness itself, the very center, which is Brahman. Abandon attachment to, and identification with, anything else. Hold to the center, yet what you are holding is what you are. It is not grasping something objective, such as an idea in the mind. Dive deep by thorough Self-Inquiry. "Who am I?" If only you pursue this inquiry deeply and consistently, such suffices for complete Realization of Brahman. **Or by subduing the mind along with the breath.** If you misidentify with them, they seem to be in control of you. If you stand free of misidentification with them, you have subdued them. Any other kind of subduing is of only temporary effect. Calming the prana, or calming the mind, it will become agitated again. If you free yourself of misidentification with such, you abide as Brahman, the true Self, and that is the lord of all. You will then become established in the heart, without misidentification. Plunging toward the center of you, through inquiry, "Who am I?" you become established in the heart. You find yourself to be Brahman, the real "I," the one Atman.

That which is innermost in you is Brahman; it is "I," the self-existent Being. It is "I-I," the self-known, quintessential Being. **Resort** to it; find your peace, your happiness, and your liberation from samsara there; find Reality and your identity there. Do so by inquiring to know the Self, and, in so inquiring, **subduing the mind,** no longer being fooled by its fancies. Subdue the mind, and subdue the senses, which function by prana, or **breath.** Be free of misidentification with the mind and its content and the prana, or animating energy, and its activities. If, inquiring, you cease to confuse yourself with the mind and its content and the prana and its activities, what will remain? **You will thus become established in the heart.** You will know the Heart, your quintessential Being, formless and absolute Brahman, as your sole identity. You do not really have another identity. This is what you are. Search for that which is most interior. If something is known by you, it is exterior to you in the spiritual sense. If you know sensations and the body, they are external to you. If you know thoughts, they are external to you. What is truly interior? This ought to be known. Pursuing inquiry in this manner is often referred to as withdrawing into the Self. From what do you withdraw? From the illusion, from misidentification. When you withdraw into the Self, you become vaster, realizing the expansive Brahman.

What is the heart? It is the center of you. **The heart-cavern,** or heart-space, is indicative of its formlessness, its boundary-less-ness, and its indivisibility. The interior of the heart-space is **the one Brahman,** for there is no multiplicity in Brahman. What do you find if you dive deep within, by any means, and find what is actually the Self, or Atman? Only Brahman. **Brahman** is expansive, immeasurably vast, truly infinite, and eternal. The center of you is what you are. Who am I? I am I, and nothing but I. Inquire within, "Who am I?" "What really am I?" It cannot be anything objective, for it is I and not an object. Knowledge of it is not an idea but the state of identity in which I am only I and not mistaken for anything else.

If one goes to the mind, there are just ideas. If one goes to the heart, there is finality. But why speak of it as "going to?" It is the place where we really are. How is this to be accomplished? It is **through Self-inquiry.** Why resort to anything else, if you can inquire? The inquiry is truly possible for all, for is there anyone who is other than the Self? Or it can be gained **by subduing the mind along with the breath.** How is the mind subdued permanently? A temporary respite will not satisfy. If one seeks the nature of the mind, the mind ceases to be the mind, and all that remains of it is pure Consciousness. If one seeks the source of the mind, it loses its form, and all that remains is pure Consciousness. **Breath** indicates prana, with which it is closely associated. We may understand prana as the animating life energy. As such, it is in control of all of the senses. The Gita instructs that one should subdue the senses, but how is one to subdue them? When you no longer regard the senses as yourself or yourself as a sensing entity and know that the reality is never determined by sensations of any kind, they are subdued. When you know yourself as the eternal, transcendent of the animating life energy, the prana is subdued. **You will thus become established in the heart.** What is this establishment? It is Knowledge. It is not an idea, but Knowledge. Not something illumined, but the Illumination itself. To abide as the Self alone and thus stand free of misidentification is to be established in the Heart. There is not so much a need to establish Knowledge, for it already is of the nature of Reality. You just need to disestablish the ignorance. If ignorance is done away with, its substrate, which is the Reality, remains. This remaining by itself is Knowledge.

Jagadishwara Shastri started writing the first three words of this verse. He could not complete the verse; he had the idea to start the verse with those three words and did not continue. While he was gone, Sri Bhagavan completed the verse. He signed the verse, as the author, as Jagadishwara. The name means Lord of the universe. So, the Lord of the universe completed the verse, and there could be no objection to it.

Verse 9

Know that awareness of and remaining as the pure, immutable Self, in the lotus of the heart, bestows Liberation, by destroying the ego.

The ego cannot stand on its own. It is a nebulous assumption with no substance. What else is the ego but the assumption that is at the root of combining what is the Self with what is not the Self? Discriminative knowledge of the pure Self is necessary.

How is one to know whether or not something is the Self? By its immutability or mutability. What changes is not the Self. What is immutable is the Self. What changes and what does not? Of this you should be keenly aware. The body changes. It cannot be the Self. The senses change. They cannot be the Self. One of the chief characteristics of the mind is its change. That cannot be the Self. If you do not falsely tie together the changeful and the changeless, where is the scope for the ego notion to flourish? If you do not misidentify the Self with the body, senses, prana, or mind, all of which are changeful, where is the place left for the ego to stand?

You should be keenly aware of your own Being existing as the changeless and remain as that. How do you remain as the Self? There are not two of you that one should remain as the other. It is a matter of interior Self-Knowledge. In practice, it manifests as a cessation of mistaking yourself to be something you are not. **Awareness of and remaining as** really are one and the same, for, in Self-Knowledge, being is knowing.

The pure, immutable Self in the lotus of the heart. Understand "heart" to mean the quintessence of your being. Remain as that. Know yourself as that. One is already That by nature. So, why imagine contrariwise? If to remain in the heart is natural, it is worthwhile to examine the causes of the illusion of wandering outside. Such is an illusion because one can never be different than the Self. You cannot separate yourself from your Existence. So, being outside the heart is an illusion. What are the illusory building blocks of that illusion? The building blocks of the illusion are just the misidentification of the Self

27

with what you cannot actually be. Inquire deeply. Inquire consistently and thoroughly. If you proceed in this manner, there comes a time when even the least deviation into illusion seems laughably absurd.

Bestows Liberation, by destroying the ego. In spiritual practice, you should do whatever is helpful for the destruction of the ego. The most direct way to bring about destruction of the ego is to seek it and see what its nature is. Attempt to track the sense of "I," the one for whom all experience appears.

It is totally within your power to identify with the sensations or not, to be attached to them or not. The senses do not have attachment built into them. The senses do not cause misidentification with them. With or without the senses, you can remain absolutely still, as unmoving Being-Consciousness-Bliss. If you mistake the senses to be who you are, if you mistake the sensations to be the reality, or if you suppose you will find your happiness through them, you will appear to wander. If you trace happiness, reality, and identity to their origin, you will not wander, and you will not move when the senses appear or when they disappear.

The senses actually do not draw you out. You imagine the outside and then imagine yourself in the outside. The sensations are innocent. They do not turn you in or out. It is entirely a matter of knowing what you truly are and not deviating from this knowledge. Deviation consists of imagining yourself to be something that you are not. The power to liberate yourself from such a tendency is entirely within your hands. There is no real obstacle to the attainment of the freedom indicated.

If you persist in an earnest inquiry to know yourself, even if the obstacles appear, they will melt before you. The obstruction is only ignorance, which is ideas in which you believe. Their strength lies in your belief. By discrimination, determine what is true. You naturally gravitate to what is true. Even if something is false, if you think it is true, you gravitate toward it. Such is delusion. Discriminate, and your own nature will draw you to itself.

The Self alone is actual experience. Everything else is merely imagined. There is no "all of it;" there is just the Self. The Self knowing the Self is direct experience. Everything else is merely imagined, or hypothetical. There may not be anything wrong in recounting your spiritual experiences, but has such worked to secure your experience? It is asking the mind to report on something that it was not there for. If it was a deeper experience, the mind was not there for it. If there were bliss, peace, freedom, and such, the essence is important. Trace the essence. Find its source and abide there. Recounting memories of the forms in which experience occurs is of dubious worth. Look for something that does not come or go. If you find that which does not come and go and which shines in its own light, you will be at the very source, the fountainhead, of all spiritual experience.

What else is the destruction of the ego but the direct perception, with keen inquiry, that the ego does not exist as such, and that all that exists, all that you are, is this one Self, which is pure, unmixed with anything else ever, and which is immutable? The Reality ever is just as it is. No change ever comes to it. It does not transform itself into something else. It is unmodified Consciousness, unmodified Being. This should be realized at the very core of you.

Every bit of bondage depends on the ego notion. Destruction of this false notion, by ceasing to accept it as real or as your identity, is freedom from every kind of bondage. In this Knowledge, what you know, you are. Awareness of and remaining as the Self of pure Existence, the Self of pure Consciousness, is liberation.

Examine and disentangle your sense of identity from "I" and "my." Be keenly aware of what, in truth, you are, and remain as that. If you seem to separate from it, ask yourself, "Who separates?" What is the definition of the one who separates? The definition is consumed in the "I." "I" is absorbed in pure Being, pure Consciousness. Thus remaining awake to your true nature is this abidance in the heart. If the misidentification as the individualized experiencer vanishes, there is a wave-less ocean of bliss.

What is **Liberation**? It is nothing but the destruction of the ego. Destruction of the ego comes about by knowing its utter unreality. If we regard it as a real thing, how will it ever be destroyed? If we discover its unreality by deep, penetrating inquiry as to who we are, it is destroyed once and for all. It is destroyed because we realize that it never existed. Such has a finality that is unmatched. Liberation is the freedom of that finality. Upon Liberation, there is no possibility of becoming bound again. One cannot become unliberated.

Destruction of the ego, which is final Liberation, is most desirable. It is the revelation of pure Being-Consciousness-Bliss. If the ego notion is destroyed, one's identity remains just as the pure Self. The **awareness**, the Knowledge of the Self and that you are That, not as a mere manner of thinking, but as direct continuous experience, is such Liberation. **Know that awareness of and remaining as the pure, immutable Self**; pure is unmixed, unalloyed, with anything else. What is your Self? Not your Self plus something else, such as a mind, a body, a subtle body, experience, memory, or anything else; what is just your Self? **Immutable**; since it is the Self, there is no question of changing into it or changing out of it. The changeless is changelessly itself. Determine what is changeless. What is ever-existent and without modification? Before birth, all during life, and after death, whether waking, dreaming, and in deep dreamless sleep, what is unchanged? Search interiorly for this. That which is unchanged is truly you. That which is mutable cannot be your actual Being. Remaining as pure Being, the pure Self, the innermost Truth of you, and free of the "I"-notion, is Liberation.

Realization is Knowledge, and, in this Realization, what you know is what you are. What is it in you, in your own experience, that is **immutable**, that never moves or changes? It is the same Consciousness that is alluded to by the description of Light. **Lotus** signifies perfection. **In the lotus of the heart**, there shines the **immutable Self. Such bestows Liberation, by destroying the ego.** How is the ego destroyed? Its destruction is by questioning it. If you question it, it will prove to be nonexistent, and such nonexistence is its destruction. What is the ego? You know the definition of it, a limited individualized being, but what actually is it? What is the sense of "I" other than the Self, or Brahman? Turning inward, by such questioning, destroys the truly nonexistent ego. It is but the barest of assumptions and survives by non-inquiry.

The attempt to flee from the ego is like running from your shadow. If you are only light, where can the shadow be? Of course, if the ego is there, there is going to be trouble. That is its only purpose, if it can be said to have one: it is to cause trouble. It is unreal, so it does not actually have a purpose.

How many selves are there for you? All of those selves cannot be the Self. You are not multiple; you are singular. Who is in need of help? What is her nature? If you inquire to know who you are, how unreal the unreal actually is becomes obvious, and, likewise, how real the Real is also becomes obvious. Just you, the one who thinks that she becomes caught in the ego, are of the nature of Liberation, if you are aware of it, which indicates Knowledge, and if you abide as it, which means that it is your Being. Consistently, thoroughly, deeply inquire to know your true nature, what you really are. Practice in such a way that your inquiry is thorough, so that neither the ego-notion nor any of the vasanas, the mental tendencies associated with it, survive. You can cut the illusion from top to bottom. All that is required is sincerity of purpose. In this way, you will not foster the ego-notion, nor give it any ground to run about on, and thus you, being Light itself, will be shadow-less. The day comes when you laugh at the illusions, the play of your own mind.

Self-inquiry is mind-transcendent. Is contemplation so? You are already the witness, pure Consciousness, which sees the rise and fall of the entire universe. Seeing whatever is going on around depends on the position, or definition, of being the body and the senses; else, how do you know about "around"? All of that is a figment of the mind. If you see all of that as one, it is perhaps better than seeing it as divided, but the best is to actually inquire to know the Self as it is, which is beyond the body, the senses, and the mind. In this way, Absolute Reality comprehends itself. If by contemplation of the One is meant absorption of one's sense of identity in that which is forever indivisible, what fault could there be in that? Contemplate the nature of the contemplator. Thereby, you will realize that which is absolutely One, and, being ever-existent, it is natural.

Verse 10

The body is inert, like a pot. Since it has no "I"-consciousness and since, in its absence in deep sleep, we still exist, it cannot be the "I." Who is it, then, that produces the feeling of "I"-ness? Where is he? In the heart-cavern of those who thus [inquire and] realize, the omnipresent Arunachala Siva shines forth of his own accord as "That-am-I" consciousness.

The body is inert, like a pot. Since it has no "I"-consciousness. The body does not produce the sense of "I." It has no knowing ability of its own. The connection of the "I" with the body, either as being a body or as being embodied, is delusion. The body is inert, but you exist and know. This "you" cannot be the body or in the body or bear the body as an attribute. Consciousness does not have the attribute of the inert. Consciousness does not dwell in the inert. Consciousness is utterly free of the inert. Just as it would be ridiculous to call a pot yourself, likewise is it to regard the body as yourself.

And since, in its absence in deep sleep, there is no bodily experience in deep, dreamless sleep, not even the thought of the body, yet **we still exist.** Therefore, **it cannot be the "I."** You exist always, even in deep, dreamless sleep. If the body were you, or were connected to you, you would never fail to have the experience of the body, and not just a part of it, but all of it. But that is the experience of no one at any time.

That we exist always is the experience of everyone. That the body does not exist in deep sleep is the experience of everyone. What conclusion can we draw from this un-contradicted experience? The conclusion is that your existence, the Self, is bodiless. If the body is inert, it does not produce the sense of "I." Who, then, **produces the feeling of "I"-ness?** From where does the identity spring? "I." From where does the feeling of "I" come?

You are led to that which is unproduced and not divided from us, but is us. That is all that we are—bodiless, egoless Existence. To undo any illusion, actually inquire. When the supposed reality of the individual "I" dissolves, where is maya?

In the heart cavern of those who thus [inquire and] realize, the omnipresent Arunachala Siva shines of his own accord, as "That-am-I" consciousness. Tracing the "I," from where it comes and what it truly is, you come to know something that is entirely bodiless, unformed, and non-individualized. It is pure Consciousness. This pure Consciousness is referred to as the omnipresent Arunachala Siva. If it is omnipresent, what form does it have, and how do you go there? The steady existence alone is your Self. It does not have a partner. Realizing the Self as the omnipresent Absolute, Siva, and that there is no other "I," the conclusive Knowledge that remains is expressed as "I-am-That." It is a statement of complete identity. The Knowledge is of the nature of Consciousness. I am that Consciousness.

The idea that there is someone to be ignorant of the Self, or who will later know the Self, is abandoned, because it is false. Echoes must have an original voice. If the original voice is I am that Consciousness, the omnipresent Siva, one silent truth of Being is resounding everywhere, and there is no one separate from this.

Trace the consciousness of "I" to its actual nature. Do not mistake the body for your Self. Do not entertain the absurd idea that the body produces your existence, as if matter produced spirit. Abandoning the misidentification with the body, based on your own irrefutable experience, trace the "I" to the heart, to the very core. No separate experiencer will remain. The significance of "I am That" will be realized. The significance is the Consciousness, itself. That alone is truly "I." Inquire and know it for certain.

The body is inert, like a pot. You would not misidentify with a pot, even if it had your name on it. So, why misidentify with this pot? It is just clay in another form. The water content is a little higher in this kind of clay. You would not think a pot is "I." You may care for a pot, and you do not intentionally destroy it, but you know it is transient, and it is not you. It is just a pot. See your body in this manner. **Since it has no "I"-consciousness**, the body does not produce the sense of "I." Whether you regard the "I" as absolute Existence or you mistakenly regard the "I" as the ego, either way, the body does not produce such. Existence is self-existent. As for the body, it does not produce it. Similarly, the body does not produce the ego notion. The body produces various substances, but it does not produce an ego.

In its absence in deep sleep. There is no experience of any kind of body in deep sleep. There is not even a memory that you had a body a few moments ago. No such thought is there. There is neither a sensation of a body nor a memory of a body, and not even the thought of a body. There is no body whatsoever in deep, dreamless sleep. Yet, you still exist and fully so. Your existence does not diminish or disappear in sleep. How, then, could the body possibly be "I"? It cannot be the "I." I am always, even in deep sleep, and the body is not there at all times, and it is inert like a pot. It is not our existence; it is not our consciousness.

If we are not bodies, what are we? **Who is it that produces the feeling of "I"-ness? Where is he?** If the feeling of "I"-ness is not produced from the body, from where does it come? "Where" does not mean a place or a location. You have the sense of "I," mistakenly individualized or the feeling without such a mistake. Where does it come from? It is not from the body.

Who am I? Where am I? Whence, from where, am I? Trace this within, relinquishing any definition that relies on the body. **In the heart-cavern**, the space of pure Being, **of those who thus [inquire and] realize, the omnipresent Arunachala Siva shines of his own accord as "That-am-I," consciousness.**

We mark the day when Sri Ramana arrived at Arunachala, who is considered the manifestation of Siva. Yet, he arrived at that which is omnipresent. How does one arrive at the omnipresent? It is Self-Knowledge. In Knowledge, the Self, which is Siva, shines of its own accord. The ego has no part of this, and the body is inert. Siva shines for Siva. The Self knows the Self. No other is involved. No other actually exists.

How does it shine forth? **As "That-am-I."** The state of identity in which Being and Knowledge are the same. The nature of this is pure Consciousness. Standing free of the tendency to misidentify with the body, deeply, continuously inquire, tracing the persistent sense of "I" inward to its very nature. That nature will shine for itself, your individuality having dropped off. Siva remains. That is the Reality, and that is what you are. That is all that there is.

The body is inert, like a pot. It has no "I"-consciousness. You are not inert. Always, you have the sense of "I". What is it? It is not the body. It is not produced by the body. It is not in the body, and it is not produced by anything in the body. To realize that you are not the body is great freedom. The body does not have the sense of "I." What is this "I"-ness? From where does it come? In ignorance, it is wrongly mixed up with the body. Discrimination shows that it is not the body. Always, you have the feeling that you exist, and the sense of "I" must have its source in the Existence. We always exist, but the body does not always appear. In deep sleep, there is no experience of the body, there is no thought about the body, and there is not even a memory of the body. You do not worry if you will get your body back when you are done sleeping. It is simply not a factor in the experience. The body is utterly absent in deep sleep, but you still exist. You exist, and you know that you exist. You do not exist as a body, and your knowledge of your Existence is not a form of thought. You do not think that you exist, no more than you think that you are without your body, in deep sleep. You do exist, bodilessly, and you know the existence. What is this existence? In what is the knowledge of it rooted? What is it that produces the feeling of "I"-ness? Trace the sense of "I" to its source.

Existence is immutable. If it ever became other than what it is, it would be destructible and would not be the Reality. In quest of the real Self, search for that which is utterly changeless. Being changeless, if it were an ego, it would be an ego for all time. Then, Liberation would be impossible, and such would mean that all of the countless sages were wrong. It is probably a much higher possibility that your mind is wrong. If it is not the ego, it never is an ego. If a rope is mistaken to be a snake in dim light, we bring a light and see that it is just a rope. It is not that a snake has just then transformed itself into a rope or that just then the snake slithered away. The rope is always there, and the snake is never there. Just so is it with the misperception of the Existence of the Self, which thinks of it in terms of an ego and the world the ego inhabits.

To the individual assumption is added various suppositions to become a thinker, an experiencer, an enjoyer, an embodied being, etc. The basic, somewhat nebulous, false assumption of existing as some kind of individual, before anything else is attributed to it, is known as the ego, or ahamkara.

There is only one "I." Discrimination is to determine the nature of the "I." The false view is that it is individualized. The true view is that it is undivided. While the two words, individualized and undivided, seem similar, there is a world of difference between them.

Who is it that produces the feeling of "I"-ness? Where is he? He is not in the body. From where does the sense of "I"-ness derive? If you trace inwardly in this manner, what happens? Sri Bhagavan declares, **In the heart-cavern**, in the space of your quintessential Being, **of those who thus [inquire and] realize**, discern the Reality as it is, **the omnipresent Arunachala Siva shines**. If Arunachala Siva is omnipresent, there is nowhere where it is not. There is, then, no space for "I" or "this," an ego or a world, because Arunachala Siva occupies the entire space, through and through. Elsewhere, in a verse, Sri Bhagavan says that A, ru and na signify Sat-Cit-Ananda, Being-Consciousness-Bliss, and their identity or oneness as That, as indicated in the declaration, "I am That," or "That you are," "Tat tvam asi." "Siva" signifies the Absolute, the supreme good, that which is wholly auspicious. Arunachala Siva is omnipresent. There is neither an ego nor a world to divide it. That One **shines**. How does it shine? Of its own accord and not by reliance on anything else. Consciousness, your real Being, is utterly non-dependent. It shines of its own accord as **"That am I" Consciousness**. The nature of Self-Knowledge is Consciousness. The Knowledge is not an idea, much less a sense-perception. Consciousness is itself the substance of this Knowledge. It is not a knowledge about something. It is pure Knowledge, for Self-Knowledge is nonobjective.

Existence will not fade. It must be known with great certainty, a certainty that can belong only to those who dive deep within, as described by Sri Bhagavan. It must be certainty beyond the mind or intellect, for they will perish or be altered, discarded or diffused, at the time of death. Verify with profound, interior certainty your freedom from the body. When it is complete, you will recognize the body as inert like an earthen pot. When a pot is created, the space in the pot is not created. When the pot moves, the space does not move. When the pot is shattered, the space is not shattered. Know the One like space to be your Self, by the keen discrimination that you are not the body. Be thorough.

You exist, and you exist always, but the body does not exist always. Not only is it transient, but it is experienced only in the waking state of mind. In deep dreamless sleep, there is no experience of a body. There is not even so much as a memory of a body, yet you exist, and your existence has not become any less for the absence of a body. The body cannot be "I." What **is it, then, that produces the feeling of "I"-ness?** There is the Self, of the nature of absolute Being, unalloyed Consciousness, and unconditional Bliss, and there appears to be a body. What is the connection between the two? The individual "I" seems to be a combination of the Being-Consciousness of the real Self and the body, but there is no such connection. If there were, it would survive in deep sleep, but it does not. Where is the one who produces the "I"-ness? It is not produced by the body. The body is inert, like an earthen pot. The Self does not produce it. The Self ever is just as it is, unborn, uncreated, and forever without modification. It can produce nothing other than its own nature, which is to say non-production. Who and how does one come in between and say "I"? If you question in this manner, the reality, the identity, returns to its rightful place, which is just the Self alone, and there is no individual to connect with the body or with anything else.

If you thus **[inquire and] realize** who you are, **the omnipresent Arunachala Siva shines forth of his own accord**. If Arunachala is omnipresent, where are you? You are only in that omnipresent One, which is in you. This shines of its own accord. How does it shine? **As Consciousness**, the Knowledge, **"That-am-I."** The Knowledge of one's identity is the Knowledge of Siva. One who meditates on Siva as different than himself should proceed deeper. To really meditate on Siva is to have one's identity absorbed in Siva. What connects the Self with the body? The body is not to be equated with the Self. The body does not produce the Self. The body is inert. Consciousness, though omnipresent, cannot be thought of as being limited to or located in a body. Consciousness, Existence, which is experienced in a manner that is timeless and location-less in deep sleep, is the Existence that is even now. This is your Existence. It is completely bodiless.

Even the false assumption, of "I," is bodiless. It is the one who says, "I could become misidentified, I fall into ignorance and thereby connect myself with the body;" implicit in that description is bodiless-ness. If even an illusion is bodiless, what can we say about the Reality?

Where is there a connection between yourself and the body? The body is born; the Self is unborn. How could you equate the two? The body is finite; the Self is infinite. How can the two be equated? The body does actions; the Self is action-less and immovable. How could the two be combined? The body perishes; the Self is eternal, ever-existent. How can the two be combined? A body appears only in the waking state of mind; the Self transcends all the states of mind. How can the two be connected? There is only an imagined connection, which is insubstantial.

If it is asked why is there such imagination, first find out "Who?" Then, you can find out "Why?" if it still exists. What is the nature of the one who makes the connection? It would be absurd to say the connection makes itself. That would suppose its preexistence.

Find out if you are a body. If you are a body, you are always a body. If you are not the body, you are never a body.

Ignorance is never caused by external circumstances. Ignorance is self-created. You cannot blame an external world for your ignorance, for the belief that there is an external world is a product of ignorance. No one and nothing forces you to be ignorant.

If ignorance had, even the least degree, its source in what is external, Liberation, or Self-Realization, would be impossible. We know from his instruction and his example that such Realization is possible. When you perceive ignorance as ignorance and nothing more, then you never comply with it. Then, you are free. Put an end to imagination, and then see what the world demands of you.

Sri Bhagavan made reference to Siva, specifically Arunachala Siva, as being omnipresent, existing everywhere. What is Siva? Siva is absolute Consciousness, inherent in which is the power to destroy all illusion and which remains by itself as the residuum of perfect Being. Meditation on Siva is accomplished in the manner of identity; that is, absolute Being-Consciousness-Bliss ought to be known as your Self.

If you inwardly determine the nature and source of happiness, you will become detached from everything else, and anger, frustration, etc., will cease to exist. For example, when you become angry, you think that something or someone has stolen your happiness, and you do not like that. It goes against your nature, because your nature is to be happy. If you knew the nature of happiness, that it is one with your existence, and if you understood that your existence is the source of happiness, it is within you, what would happen to the anger? The anger that you felt would dissipate, and new anger would no longer be produced. The same holds true of all the other emotions, which are nothing more than recurring thoughts. The only true feeling is Bliss. It also manifests as love, which is the indivisibility of real Being.

Verse 11

He alone is born who, after inquiring, "Where was I born?" is born in his source, which is Brahman. Know that he is ever-born and daily renewed. He is the supreme sage.

From where is the "I" born? There can be only one true source. It is Brahman. If you find that the "I" is only in and of Brahman, your experience of bliss is **daily renewed**, ever fresh; it never grows old. The Self's fascination with itself, characterized by supreme bliss, never becomes stale and never decays. This is unlike anything else. Everything else wears thin. This never wears out. If only this is known, there is perfection.

Through imagination, you are born in illusion. Through Knowledge, you are born in Brahman.

One should find one's source. Where was I born? From where does the sense of "I" spring? Trace this to its source, and, figuratively, you are born there. Where is "there"? Brahman.

Know that he is ever-born. Being is most ancient. It is timeless, and it never grows old. Likewise is the realization of the Self. It is timeless, and it never grows old. It is ever-born. The bliss of the Self never grows stale. The Knowledge of the Self remains of perpetual fascination.

He is the supreme sage. What is a sage? He is someone who is wise, who has realized the Self. What is a sage? He does not have the thought that he is a sage. What is he? Who is Bhagavan? We know him as our beloved, very dear sadguru, but who is he? What is he? Those who have realized and the sadguru are "personal, impersonal Brahman." You may see him as a sage, but what he really is, through and through, is Brahman, and he has no mistake regarding his identity. He shows that to us, and we, similarly, become ever-born, in Brahman. We do not remain as a plurality. With the ego gone, individuality effaced, we can say in the deepest sense there is only one supreme sage, just as there is only one Brahman and no multiplicity at any time. If you think in terms of bodies, you will think that this statement means that he is a unique individual. What he is, though, is Brahman, which is indivisible and undifferentiated, and anyone who is born there becomes that utterly, with not a trace left over; so there is only one.

Trace the "I" to its source. To be born is to awaken to your source. It seems as if you are tracing your source, but, upon doing so, you find it is actually what you are; what you are is the source of what you take yourself to be. **He is ever-born and daily renewed**. Self-Realization, though it is the ancient state, never grows old. What grows old? The body grows old. What grows old? Sensations grow old. What grows old? Thinking grows old, and that quickly so. What does not grow old? Finding your Self, you find that which is ever-fresh yet most ancient. Only one who knows and is the Self is a **supreme sage**. Knowledge about anything else grows old. Knowledge of That, what you are, never grows old. The Self remains of perpetual fascination because of its Bliss, because of its unconceived nature, and because it is the very nature of Reality, the perfectly full.

What is your **source**? The sense of "I" arises. What is its source? If the source is Brahman, does anything other than Brahman come forth from it? If Brahman alone comes forth from Brahman, has anything really come forth at all? Inquire and find this by direct experience. Direct experience of the Self is ever fresh; your Existence never wears thin. Mere thinking is dead. Direct experience is ever new, ever fresh, though ancient and always the same. If we consider this description in terms of thoughts and objects, it is difficult to make sense of it. How could you be ever born and ancient simultaneously? Your Being is eternal, timelessly the same, yet ever new, ever sparkling fresh. Bliss does not decay.

Verse 12

Give up the idea that this loathsome body is the Self. Realize the eternally blissful Self. To seek to know the Self while cherishing the ephemeral body is like mistaking a crocodile for a log and trying to cross the river on it.

Give up the idea that the body is the Self. It is actually the misidentification with the body that is loathsome. The body is inert. To regard yourself as such an inert thing is to be loathed, because bondage is unnatural and breeds all kinds of suffering. If you wish to realize the eternally blissful Self, you must abandon the tendency to identify with the body. If you carry the body-misidentification with you in the attempt to realize the Self, this is comparable to stepping on the back of a crocodile, thinking that it is a log, and trying to cross a river on it. What are the chances of reaching the other shore? You will go partway and then be pulled under. This is not the way to proceed. One should disidentify from the body. Indeed, the gateway to spiritual experience truly opens when one has left behind the misidentification with the body. Until then, there are just preparations for the journey, but one is not actually crossing the river.

To give up the misidentification with the body, all you need do is examine your existence. What is it? That will suffice.

Knowledge reveals that which the senses cannot. The purpose of the instruction and the path of jnana, or Knowledge, is to reveal reality, to reveal that which cannot be apprehended by any other means, such as through the senses or through the mere thinking of the intellect. Do not take the crocodile tour. Your true nature is free, and you are always free to discover this freedom. There are really no obstacles in your path. If, though, you insist on an attempt to absorb an infinite Knowledge in a limited vessel, there will be some difficulty. It will not fit. If you abandon the walls of that vessel, it will fit nicely. Space pours itself into space. Such is the absorption in Truth. There is something to be known about ignorance: it is not necessary. There is another thing to know about ignorance: it is not true.

The body is **ephemeral**, transitory, lasting for but a brief moment in time. What you seek to realize is eternal and infinite. The finite cannot realize the infinite. The transitory cannot realize the eternal. Inquire and thereby relinquish the misidentification with a transitory thing, and find yourself safely on the other shore of the Realization of Brahman.

"To identify oneself with the body and yet to seek happiness is like attempting to cross a river on the back of an alligator." (Talks with Sri Ramana Maharshi, #396, April 12, 1937)

The reference to the crocodile is from Adi Sankara. He compares the body to a crocodile. If you climb aboard for a ride, what is going to happen, sooner or later? In the quest for Self-Realization, one is attempting to reach the other shore by crossing over the river of samsara, the ocean of samsara, of birth, death, and illusion. How could the body be a fit vessel for doing so? No one would climb on a crocodile, thinking this is a good log, and use it as a raft to cross a river, because of the consequences. Equally absurd is it to carry the misidentification with the body and attempt to realize the Self. Your spiritual practice should not be body-bound but should partake of the same bodiless freedom as the Self that you are trying to realize.

Give up the idea that this loathsome body is the Self. The body is really neutral, but if you regard it as the Self, such a state is loathsome. Realize the eternally blissful Self. Who can

42

describe the happiness of the Self? You have to find it for yourself, by turning within and abandoning the misidentification with the body.

How much of suffering is based on misidentification with the body? Without this ignorant misidentification, how great, deep, and lasting is your happiness? You will not be satisfied with anything less than eternal happiness. Desire will continue to arise until the eternal happiness is found and realized conclusively, because it is your very nature, and you cannot be satisfied with anything less than what you are. If your aim is to realize the Self as eternal, will you look to the body as a definition for yourself? Holding the Self to be the body is like mistaking the crocodile for a log.

Give up the idea that the body is the Self and **realize the eternally blissful Self.** To whatever degree you misidentify with the body, to that degree you appear to be bound and suffer needlessly. To the degree you remain free from the body misidentification, to that degree you are free of bondage and suffering. If the misidentification with the body is given up entirely, by knowing that it is just a misidentification, a mistake and not the truth, the bondage and suffering due to the misidentification become quite impossible. If you want to cross the river of transmigration, the cycle of samsara, birth and death and illusion, and you seek support for your spiritual practice in order to do so, do not grasp the crocodile-log of the "I am the body" misconception. If you do, you will drown in the attempt. Do not practice in a way that is based on the "I am the body" misconception, but practice in a way that dissolves that misconception. Action of the body does not lead to Liberation; Knowledge alone does so.

Relinquishment of the idea that the body is the Self is possible. You do it effortlessly every night in deep sleep. Seeking to realize the Self and retaining the "I am the body" conception just will not work.

The shrinkage of the distance between Bhagavan and you is proportionate to the subsidence of the ego. When you pray to him, he, being identical with God, already knows what it is for which you are praying. The answer is there before the question. The help and support are there, even before the prayer.

43

The prayer causes the ego to diminish, and then you say that his presence returns. You need not concoct a theory of lila, in order to describe your experience. You can set about causing a reduction of the ego directly; such is spiritual practice. Since his presence is of an absolute nature, it is ridiculous to ascribe to him any lila or similar attribute. You are having a rough journey while sailing on a mirage. Recognize the mirage for what it is, and the difficulties are over. Realize his presence is always there, and your difficulties are over.

Ignorance does not have a real starting place. It seems to have its origin in the "I"-notion. The "I" notion comes first. Who is entrapped in it? The same "I." How can a notion be trapped in itself? That is how illusion appears. Ignorance does not necessarily make sense. Because it is not due to external causes, there is the availability of Self-Realization for all. Bhagavan's spiritual instruction and Grace have made it the easiest thing there is.

Cherishing the ephemeral body. By **cherishing** is meant regarding it as "I" or as "mine." As long as the misidentification with the body continues, just so long illusion continues. Severance of the "I am the body" conception, the destruction of that misidentification, is so important.

Verse 13

Gifts, penance (tapas), sacrifice, upright conduct (dharma), self-control (yoga), devotion (bhakti), heaven (the expanse of Consciousness), substance (existence), peace, truth, grace, silence, the supreme state, deathless death, knowledge, renunciation, Liberation, bliss— know that all these are only severance of the I-am-the-body consciousness.

Gifts. In the spirit of giving there is, to a greater or lesser degree, the severance of the I-am-the-body consciousness. There is some disappearance of the definitions separating the giver and the one who receives. Severance of the I-am-the-body mentality is a blessed gift, and any kind of giving depends, at least to a certain degree, on loss of that body-centered mentality. If, by gifts, the allusion is to the giving to God and to the holy, as enjoined by the Vedas and others, the abandonment of the misidentification with the body is the complete fulfilment of such.

Penance. The meaning of tapas is also intense, fiery practice. Severance of the I-am-the-body consciousness is intense, fiery practice. Cut off the illusory, deluded connection that ties the self to the body.

Sacrifice. The real sacrifice to be made, the one that results in lasting good, is the cutting off of the egoistic notion of being a body. This is the sacrifice that should be poured into the fire of Knowledge. The dissolution of the misidentification with the body is the purpose and essence of worship.

Upright conduct. Dharma is the path of righteousness or that which pertains to one's own nature. Freedom from the I-am-the-body misconception is natural for you. This is the right path, dharma.

Self-Control. Yoga means union. Divine union with the Absolute comes only by severance of the I-am-the-body misconception. If the I-am-the-body misconception is gone, where is the separation? There is natural union.

Devotion. Bhakti is the dissolution of the ego, the sweet surrender that involves the destruction of the I-am-the-body misconception.

Heaven (the expanse of Consciousness). How is one to abide in it? It is not by death of the body but by death of the I-am-the-body misconception.

Substance (existence). Existence is by nature bodiless. One who ceases to misidentify with the body realizes himself as Existence, the one substance that actually is.

You do not actually become a body. You do not actually enter into a body. There is no place in the body where you are. If part of the body is lost, you do not cease to exist, and you do not diminish. You are neither in it nor spread all over it. You are just not it. Only the body is in pain. The "I" is not in pain, and one who knows this does not suffer on any account. Pain and pleasure, like life and death, are seen with an equal eye. The revelation of all that is true, good and beautiful involves the disidentification with the body.

45

Peace. Without ceasing to misidentify with the body, how will one know peace? If you relinquish the misidentification with this transitory body, you become peace. You are not just peaceful; you are the peace.

Truth. Realization of the truth while retaining the I-am-the-body misconception is quite impossible. Once the I-am-the-body misconception is relinquished, truth cannot be hidden but shines as your own Being, self-known and ever-existent.

Grace. What greater grace could there be than freedom from the bodily confines? By grace, one is freed of the terrible misconception "I am the body." Being free from that, what remains is not an embodied state but a state of grace without bounds.

Silence. If you sever the I-am-the-body misconception, what remains is silent Being, the unspeakable, the unthinkable, and quite bodiless.

The supreme state. With a body, one appears to be caught in limitation. Free from the body, what are your limits? Can a body realize that which is infinite and eternal? Can one who identifies himself with the body realize the infinite and the eternal, the supreme state? Give up the idea "I am the body," and the supreme state is your own. You, yourself, are the infinite and the eternal. The supreme state is the innate one.

Deathless death. It is death of the egoistic notion "I am the body." You do not cease to exist with the end of the body, and you most certainly do not cease to exist with the end of the confusion regarding the body. The confusion posits your identity as being a body. Was not this deathless death the Maharshi's experience, sometimes referred to by devotees as his "death experience"? He did not die, but the false connection with the body died. It was a deathless death, and blissful immortality remained thereafter.

Knowledge. Where ignorance disappears, Knowledge shines. How much ignorance is dependent on the wrong idea of "I am the body"?

Renunciation. If one retains the "I-am-the-body" misconception and merely abstains from objects that are in close proximity to the body, what actually has been accomplished? Possession of objects is determined by whether or not they are

46

in the vicinity. In either case, if there is severance of the "I-am-the-body" misconception, there is no bondage, and that is the true spirit of renunciation. It is the deep nonattachment that comes from being bodiless, which is the essence and real meaning of renunciation.

Liberation. Since the "I-am-the-body" misconception is foundational to ignorance, and ignorance is bondage, for liberation from bondage, there is no other way but severance of the misconception of being a body. If you relinquish the misidentification with the body, you find happy liberation from all bondage. You find that all bondage, just like the bondage to the body, is unreal, and thus you are set free. This results in **bliss**. With the misidentification with the body, there is suffering. Freedom from misidentification is the destruction of suffering.

In order to bear fruit, every spiritual means employed depends on the severance of the "I-am-the-body" concept. With the misidentification with the body, there appears bondage. Set free of misidentification with the body, liberation is at hand.

The Self is not the body. If you realize that you are not the body, the distinction between the giver and the given vanishes and, in this is found the true gift. If you realize that you are not the body, this is true tapas, the intense, fiery practice that yields Liberation. Truly, **tapas** is bodiless. When the Upanishad says, "Tapas is Brahman," that which is referred to as tapas is freedom from misidentification, such as the "I am the body" concept. What is to be sacrificed? The "I am the body" conception. The realization that you are not the body is the sacrifice to be made. You do not sacrifice the body; you sacrifice the "I am the body" concept. What is to be reached by worship is freedom from the "I am the body" conception. **Dharma**, what is truly one's own dharma, is freedom from the misidentification with the body. **Yoga** is union with the bodiless Self. Freedom from the body is truly yoga, union, and the means to attain such. Freedom from the misconception of being the body is of the very essence of **devotion**, and devotion is entirely bodiless. Freedom from the misidentification with the body is the realization of the expanse of Consciousness, and that is truly heaven. **Heaven, or the expanse of Consciousness**, is the state in which the "I am the body" notion no longer prevails. Free from misidentification with the body is the real substance, the real **Existence**. Freedom from misidentification with the body is peace. So long as you remain misidentified with the body, how can you have peace, let alone experience it permanently? If you know that you are not the body, peace is always there. **Peace** is to be reached by freedom from the "I am the body" concept. If you are free of the misidentification with the body, what can disturb your peace? The fact that you are not the body is Truth. **Truth** is entirely bodiless. Freedom from misidentification with the body is a state of grace, and **Grace** transcends the body entirely. Freedom from misidentification with the body is silence. Silence is not mere bodily quietude. Silence is the egoless state found by disidentifying from the body. **Silence** is entirely bodiless. Freedom from the "I am the body" supposition is the supreme state, for it is blissful immortality, beyond which there is nothing else. The **supreme state** signifies the Knowledge of Reality. If a connection, of "I" and "mine," in relation to the body, remains, it is not the supreme state. Freedom from misidentification with the body reveals the supreme state to be innate. Freedom from misidentification with the body is **deathless death**. What dies? The "I am the body" misconception dies. You do not die. You are forever. It is severance of the "I am the body" consciousness that is known as deathless death. The "I am the body" misconception, the ego, dies. Real Being never perishes. Freedom from the "I am the body" misidentification is **Knowledge**. Without this freedom, where is Knowledge? That misidentification is the very cornerstone of ignorance, and the destruction of ignorance is the shining forth of true Knowledge. If there is misidentification with the body, whatever one thinks is certainly not Knowledge. If there is freedom from the "I am the body" concept, with inner peace and happiness experienced always, such is Knowledge. What is to be renounced? Renunciation of objects can take one only so far. Freedom from misidentification with the body is truly renunciation. Giving up things is only partial **renunciation**. Giving up attachment to them is better. Then, the detachment should be directed toward the body, so that one ceases to be misidentified with the body; this is the best. If the misidentification with the body is renounced, one's renunciation is complete, and one is free from samsara. It is **Liberation** and **bliss**. Such freedom is known as Liberation, and the experience of being bodiless is Bliss itself. What are all of these? Simply the **severance of the I-am-the-body consciousness.**

Do not desire the body. Do not hate it. Do not take it to be yourself. It is just a body; it is not you. Who are you? With transcendence over the body, you find yourself to be the Truth that is revealed. To abide in such bodiless Being, all that is necessary is to deeply inquire, "Who am I?" It is not that you are a body and spiritual practice makes you disembodied. Even now, and always, you are not the body. Knowledge is the recognition of the fact. Inquire so this Knowledge shines for you.

Verse 14

To inquire who it is who has karma, vibhakti (lack of devotion), viyoga (separation), and ajnana (ignorance) is the true path of karma, bhakti, yoga, and jnana. Remaining as the Self, which has none of these things, and without an ego to make the inquiry is, indeed, the true state.

To be entirely free of the misidentification of being the performer of any action is the significance of karma yoga. When, having relinquished the idea of being the body, you question if you are the actor, are you the doer, you find that you are not the performer of any action, but you exist as bodiless Being-Consciousness-Bliss. **To inquire who it is who has the karma,** who has the action, is the way to achieve peace. To realize within that the one who is lacking in devotion does not exist as such, inquiring, "For whom is **vibhakti?** For whom is **lack of devotion?"** the ego notion vanishing entirely, is parabhakti, the supreme devotion, in which nonduality shines.

If one is seeking yoga, or union with God, with the Absolute, to question, "Who has **viyoga,** non-union, or **separation?"** and to thus discover the absence of the ego is, indeed, the attainment, as well as the practice, of yoga. If yoga is considered to be the conquest of the mind and other faculties in order to reach the divine, to inquire as to the nature of the supposed possessor of these and find yourself to be utterly attributeless, free of any of the mind and other faculties, is, indeed, yoga, union, because of one's identity as solely being the Absolute, or Brahman.

The true path of jnana, which results in jnana, Knowledge, is to inquire who it is that could entertain or possess ignorance. Who is the one who is ignorant? Since Knowledge is knowledge of the Self, who is it that claims not to know the Self? If you claim that you do not know the Self or do not abide as the Self, it is imperative to question who the "I" is that supposedly does not know the Self. To realize the nonexistence of the ego, the one who could be ignorant, the root of ignorance, is the utter annihilation of all ignorance, and this is the illuminative path of knowledge and the result, which is also Knowledge.

Remaining as the Self, which has none of these things, no action, no lack of devotion, no separation, and no ignorance. To remain as that is to identify yourself as being solely the Self and not the individual at all, and **without an ego to make the inquiry, is, indeed, the true state.** Who is the inquirer? The Self cannot be realized in an objectified manner. The way is nonobjective.

If you assume the stance of an individual, as if that is the nature of the inquirer, the inquiry should be into that very one, in order to realize the nonexistence of the individuality, or ego. If the "I" is the Self, such is **the true state** and is the vast expanse of pure Consciousness, the real Knowledge. If the "I" is individualized, what is the nature of that one? Who is it that inquires? The inquiry consists of luminous Knowledge that is inherent in Consciousness alone.

However the path is conceived, the nonexistence of the individual, the realization of egolessness, is the essence and the fruit. Inquiry consists in the destruction of the notion of an inquirer, leaving the residuum of pure Consciousness, Knowledge, which is actually the essence of the inquiry. If you question the very existence of the individuality, being unreal, it vanishes, leaving true Being that is complete.

Sri Bhagavan removes the definition of the one who is not devoted. He removes the idea of viyoga, separation. Then, what remains of the yogi? What remains of the bhakta? The question is, does the "I" exist as such? If you set about an inquiry into that, there will be no separation but only the innate union. Where there is only one, how could there be separation? What would separate from what? Question the idea of the individuality of the inquirer. Who is this "I"? If he is considered separate from the Self, he is unreal. How else would you get rid of the individual except by examining whether it is real? If it proves to be unreal, it is already gone.

Everything can be seen to prove your freedom, rather than the purported validity of bondage or ignorance. The perception of any vasana is just one more thing of which you are free. The realized state is the only state there actually is, and the quest for Self-Knowledge is not so much an addition of a new state to oneself, but the removal of the false belief in a second state, an unrealized state, which is an illusion.

The Self does not have karma, lack of devotion, separation, or ignorance. Who does? Who has karma? Who has separation? Who lacks devotion? Who has ignorance? Inquire. The individual who seems to commence the inquiry, or appears at its beginning, is destroyed in the process of inquiry.

Paths are spoken of in reference to an ego. The path of karma is spoken of in order to reduce or destroy the ego. The path of devotion is spoken of to destroy the ego to realize the egoless Supreme. Yoga is spoken of, as if a separation has occurred, so that union might be achieved, which is the destruction, or disappearance, of the ego. Jnana, knowledge, is spoken of to undo the ignorance that is the ego. Does the ego exist? Even if you assume that it does, if you thus inquire, "For whom is this ignorance? For whom is this separation? For whom is the karma?" and such, there will be found to be no one there by the name of "I." Just the pure Self exists. That in which there is no ego and in which even the inquiry is resolved is your true state. That is the natural state.

Do not treat meditation as if it were an event or an experience that belonged to somebody. That which appears in the form of inquiry is the Knowledge itself. Consider this and the preceding verse together. Sever the "I-am-the-body concept" and inquire "Who am I?" so deeply that even the idea of an individual inquirer is destroyed.

Thinking "I am ignorant" prompts one to seek knowledge. Seeking knowledge, one must inquire. Inquire into the one for whom the ignorance is. Then, one finds that ignorance does not exist anymore. Inquire, even now, what is the truth regarding you? What can you think about yourself? Is this thought you? It is neither you nor your possession. Where would any bondage be? Where would any ignorance be? The forms of the ignorant concepts are gone, and the idea that you possess them is also gone. Both the ignorance and the one who is ignorant are unreal. What is the truth regarding your existence? Consciousness is not ignorant.

There is the division between ignorance and knowledge only so long as the ego appears. Inquiring into who the ego, "I," is, the form of ignorance vanishes. The state of ignorance is no more. The ignorant one turns out to be nonexistent. There are not two selves. Only one Self is, and the Self is of the very nature of Knowledge. Knowledge does not become ignorant at any time. Because this is so, there is permanence in liberation, which is freedom from the imagined bondage. If, in reality, the ignorant state existed, even after dispensing with it, it might return. There would be no eternal liberation; but there is, indeed, eternal liberation. It is the very nature of your Self.

You are not a self who is ignorant of the Self. Rather, the one Self exists, and you are that. The practice of inquiry destroys the notion of a second self, an "I." The inquiry destroys it because it never actually exists.

By inquiring, "Whose is karma, for whom is separation, for whom is ignorance, and for whom is lack of devotion?" the false sense of individuality dissolves. What is the true path to Self-Realization, regardless of the form of the approach, such as these described? The true path to Self-Realization always involves the disappearance of the ego assumption. By whatever means such is accomplished, it is beneficial. What better means could there be than inquiring to determine what "I" really signifies?

Remaining as the Self, which has none of these things. The Self does not have separation from itself. Who does? The Self does not have lack of devotion to itself. So, who does? The Self is undoubtedly free of all action and all karma.

So, who is enmeshed in such? The Self has no ignorance. So, who is it that appears to be ignorant? The Self is also One without a second. For That there is no "another." So, how can any ignorance and such actually exist? **Without an ego to make the inquiry is, indeed, the true state.** An ego is non-existent; it is utterly unreal. How can that which is unreal inquire? The Self is of the nature of pure, absolute Knowledge. The Self has no need of an inquiry. It is only from the perspective of existing as an individualized self that inquiry becomes absolutely necessary, in order to attain the realization of the pure Self as it is, in which there is no trace of individuality. The instruction should not be misconstrued to formulate the idea that the ego is an actual entity or has a power to inquire. The ego is not an entity, has no actual existence, and has no power to do anything. How could the unreal accomplish? If you suppose yourself to be an individual, there is the need to inquire. Having inquired, "Who am I?" what remains? Just the one Self, the absolute Being-Consciousness-Bliss, in which there is not the least possibility of ignorance, remains. Then, there is no need for an inquiry; there is nothing to be clarified. The Knowledge, which manifests as the inquiry, remains unmixed, infinite and endless. This Knowledge is of the nature of absolute Consciousness. This is, indeed, the true state. The state of being individualized is not the truth. The state of ignorance, of separation, of lack of devotion, karma, etc., is not the true state. What is your true state? Your true state is Being, Being alone, Being just as it is.

To whom do ignorance, division or separation, lack of devotion, and karma or action pertain? If you inquire, the distinction of these vanishes, because they are not the reality. The one who supposedly has them proves to be also unreal. It is in our very nature to abide in what is real. So, what is real? As long as the unreal, or not-Self, seems to be, so long inquiry should be carried out in fullness. When neither an unreal subject nor an unreal object remain, the form of inquiry vanishes, and all that remains is the vast expanse of true Knowledge, which is Being-Consciousness-Bliss. Note that you never put an end to the inquiry; the inquiry puts an end to the so-called "you." The real nature of the inquiry turns out to be unformed, imperishable

Knowledge. That also is your only true Self, the only Self that there is.

Verse 15

The attitude of those mad men who, without realizing the power that animates them, expect to attain all supernatural powers, reminds one of the story of the lame man who said, "If I am supported on my feet, what can the enemy do?"

The realization of Truth is not about acquiring extraordinary or exceptional powers with the body, with the prana, or with the mind. This point can be expanded to the idea of some kind of personal power of any kind. The idea that the individual holds some power is like the lame man saying if he is held up, he will defeat the entire enemy. It is absurd.

What props up the individual? The individual cannot stand by its own power. To think that one would enhance the individual by one's spirituality is absurd. So, he says **mad.** There is one power that is everywhere. One should abide at the root of it, and this abidance means the disappearance of one's individuality. The ability to perceive the future, the minds of others, and such is just more knowledge of illusion. A power displayed in a dream is no real power at all. To wake up from the dream, so as not to be entangled in samsara, is real power. This is the power of Self-Knowledge. It is not an acquisition for the individual, but the dissolution of the individuality.

The analogy expresses the absurdity. By what power is all this? All is supported and appears by one supreme power. Creation, sustenance, and destruction belong to it alone. What power does the individual have, in light of the fact that the individual does not exist? There is one supreme power. To attribute any kind of power to one's so-called self is absurd. It is a kind of worldly ignorance that thinks the attainment of extraordinary powers belongs to the realm of the spiritual. Such need not be supernatural, miraculous powers. Such may be pride in one's intellectual powers, one's physical powers, one's financial powers, or one's political powers. The ego is so small; it is actually unreal. What power does it have? To think, "I am here," is delusion. To think, "I am here, and I have some power," is double delusion. Far better is it to happily rest peacefully knowing that there is one supreme power. It is universal.

In the analogy, the lame person has assumed an absurd, egotistical perspective. The idea of being an embodied individual is ignorance. To equate spiritual advancement with some sort of extraordinary powers of the body, the subtle body, or of the mind is the same absurd position of thinking one is an embodied individual. There is no spiritual advancement or Self-Realization in such. There is one power that supports all. It is the Existence, or God. One should not conceive of the spiritual height as being a form, state, or attribute of a body, gross or subtle. No matter what extraordinary abilities or powers one may appear to have, and that can be only in a transitory fashion, such cannot compare to one who has realized that he has no power of his own, no individuality of his own, and who rests as the omnipotent Existence, itself. Understand that what you seek in spiritual realization and by spiritual practice is not a larger or more important "you," but rather your disappearance, the disappearance of "I" and "mine," so that absolute Being, the Self, alone remains. Trace the power by which this entire universe, inclusive of your body and lifetime, appears to its source. That is deep and enduring.

The individual does not actually exist. So, what of his attributes, even if they be extraordinary ones, can be real? It is in the disappearance of individuality that the Supreme is realized. Understood in this manner, we comprehend that the glorious reality is not that the Maharshi was an extraordinary individual, though he may appear that way, but that in him there was not the least trace of individuality whatsoever, and all that remained of him was That.

That in which you are bodiless and egoless is your natural state. You never actually become a body. Misidentification does not really connect you with the body. Bodiless Being is simply the fact. You have not been young; you are not now older. You were not born; you will not die. You do not become active, nor do you become inactive. You do not have ordinary abilities; you do not have extraordinary abilities. The body is not the Self. To realize bodiless Being as it is is the purpose of spirituality. Sri Bhagavan equates those who conceive of spirituality as a means of enhancing the abilities of the body with madmen. Spirituality is for nothing less than Liberation, which is eternal Self-Realization. To neglect that and put one's efforts into enhancing some peculiar attribute or ability of the body is craziness.

Liberation is the severance of the "I am the body" consciousness. Consider how much ignorance and bondage rest upon the "I am the body" misconception. Without that one piece of ignorance, where would the bondage be? The relinquishment of it naturally brings transcendence of the senses and transcendence of all the thoughts of the mind that have the "I am the body" misconception woven into them. There is tremendous freedom in this. It is also great wisdom.

What you are in quest of is bodiless. It is freedom from the misidentification with the body and not the attainment of some unusual bodily abilities. Similarly, it is to be free of misidentification with the prana and the mind and not the engagement in some unusual phenomena of the mind and prana. One power moves all. The power should be known at its source. The Reality is the ultimate power. Realization of it is the highest attainment, because it is real. Reality itself is the supreme power, for there is nothing else than it over which to have power.

Verse 17

The Lord bears the burden of the world. The pseudo-self, which thinks it bears it, is like the grinning sculpted figure (at the foot of a temple tower) that seems to support it. Whose fault is it if one who travels in a cart carries the luggage on his head to his own discomfort, instead of putting it in the cart, which carries it anyway?

D.: What is Self-surrender?

M.: It is the same as self-control; control is effected by removal of samskaras, which imply the functioning of the ego. The ego submits only when it recognizes the Higher Power. Such recognition or surrender is submission or self-control. Otherwise, the ego remains stuck up like the image carved on a tower making a pretense by its strained look and posture that it is supporting the tower on its shoulders. The ego cannot exist without the Power, but thinks that it acts of its own accord....

A passenger in a train keeps his load on his head by his own folly. Let him put it down; he will find the load reaches the destination all the same. Similarly, let us not pose as the doers, but resign ourselves to the guiding power. (Talks with Sri Ramana Maharshi, 398, April 14, 1937)

What burdens do you have? What are you carrying? All of one's concerns, fears, anxieties, and worries are equivalent to holding the luggage on top of one's head, giving one an awful headache. What carries the entire load, anyway? What is it that carries this entire universe, with every detail of your life included? The "I" that seems to creep in in delusion and thinks anxiously that it is burdened and the performer of action is like the sculptured figure in the temple tower. It is sculpted to appear as if it were holding up the tower, but, of course, it is not. The tower rests entirely on its foundations. The sculpted figure is in a bas relief and has no existence apart from the stone out of which it is carved. It is similar to the individual and his idea of carrying anything. He does not have a separate existence and does not bear the burden of the world.

The idea of the power of the individual is entirely illusory. There is really not a strong individual or a weak individual. There is no individual. One power upholds or manifests everything. If we understand this, we remain tranquilly detached. Note that this is not an attitude of being resigned to circumstances. It is a far vaster view of one indivisible Existence, one God, one power, with nothing existent contrary to it. A mental attitude of resignation to circumstances while retaining the "I" and the I-am-the-body concepts is mere delusion. One power carries all. If you think that you are carrying, that power is also carrying you, just like the person in the cart holding the luggage. The luggage and the person are both being carried in the cart. Know that which underlies all and supports all, and have your identity become absorbed in that.

One power pervades, supports, and rules this entire universe. Happy is it to recognize that. This recognition yields de-

tachment and freedom from the false concept of being the performer of action.

**The pseudo-self, which thinks it bears the it, "is like
the grinning sculpted figure (at the foot of a temple
tower) that seems to support it.** The sculpted figure does
not support anything. It is just an image on the surface. Likewise
is the pseudo-self, the supposed ego or individual who thinks
that it is in charge, bears the burden and suffers needlessly.

**Whose fault is it if one who travels in a cart carries
his luggage on his head to his own discomfort, instead
of putting it in the cart, which carries it anyway?** There
is great delight in knowing that you never do anything. Either
discern clearly that you are not the body, so it is not possible
for you to do anything, or recognize that there is one supreme
power of which the body is one of countless instruments, all
wielded by the same power from beginning to end. In either
case, no scope is left for the delusion of an ego. Where the ego
is not, suffering is not.

In truth, no one is a body. All are the real Self, infinite Being-
Consciousness-Happiness, but, thinking that they are bodies,
they suffer. They suffer needlessly. The suffering seems as if real,
but lasts only so long as the I-am-the-body misconception continues. When that misconception is abandoned, the cause of
suffering is gone, and the suffering, itself, proves to be unreal,
much like the experiences seen in last night's dream. To see the
needlessness of suffering and to perceive the real Self, transcendent of the body and its actions, is the root of compassion. The
compassion is not only feeling that the suffering is needless, but
it also resolves itself into the state of identity. So, it is no longer
a means of relating to someone, but the unity of Existence. This
is just blissful Being.

It is worthwhile to wonder what the experience would be, if
all of the suffering and hallucinations based on the I-am-the-
body concept were wiped away. The idea of location would be
gone, the ideas of birth and death would be gone, and the ideas
of doing anything at any time would be gone. The idea of being
in time and space would be gone. The idea of being in a world
would be gone. The idea that there is an external world would
be gone. Dive deep into this non-identification with the body.

If you liberate yourself from false definition, true Knowledge will shine from within.

Intensely direct your inquiry, again and again, deeper and deeper, until you discern that you are not the body and the I-am-the-body misconception cannot possibly return. Then, you are free. One-pointedness implies no distinction between the inquirer and what he is inquiring into, the meditator and that upon which he meditates.

The Lord, who is none other than the Self, is the Reality. Reality does not need any assistance from the ego to prop it up. The one Existence, which is the one power, is self-established. If you assume that you are in charge and act, such is illusion. If you travel in a conveyance, such as a cart, and place your luggage on your head, as if that were the means of carrying it, that would be absurd. The conveyance is actually doing all of the carrying, carrying your body as well as the luggage. Likewise is it with your life. Who is the support of it? What great power carries all? That power by which the entire universe appears and disappears determines your life, as well. To claim some small speck as you and yours is delusion.

The figure sculpted into the temple tower is made to appear as if it is holding up the entire tower. This can be seen at Adi Annamalai temple, where such a figure is carved into the gopuram, the temple tower. The figure that is carved into the tower does not really exist as such. The substance of the tower is the only thing that is there, and the tower rests firmly on its foundation. The figure is not real, and his activity, strength, power, and his holding up the tower are not real either. Just so is it with the ego and its so-called activities. The ego is not real, and it is not in charge of anything. Therefore, there should not be any doubt concerning how will everything get on without your ego, but the question should be, "How did anything get on with an ego?"

When Bhagavan rubbed some liniment into his arthritic knees to make them function better and to relieve the pain, did that bring about misidentification for him? To think it did would be absurd. All the power lies in Knowledge and not in a specific action. The physical maintenance of the body does not represent bondage. Thinking that the body is you, that you are in it, and that it is your possession should be eliminated. This is the cure for samsara.

The supreme Lord carries all and is in charge of all. The idea that the individual, on its own, is accomplishing this thing or that thing is far-fetched. In the analogy, there is a sculptured figure at the base of a tower of a temple. The figure has no existence apart from the stone of the temple tower. It is just a carved figure, and not a real figure, made to appear as if it is supporting the entire tower. It is absurd. The ego has no separate existence apart from God and has no power, for all power belongs to God. If you think it is your doing, you will pile troubles in your mind, like carrying the luggage on your head, in the second analogy. The cart carries all anyway. Just so, when you carry the worries of your life and the worries of the world with you, it is farcical. It is suffering to no purpose. If God is, God is everywhere at all times. There is no scope for the individual or the individual's power. Retire from the sense of doership.

Verse 25

Through constant, uninterrupted meditation in the heart, "That Consciousness, which is devoid of all adjuncts, that Siva, I am," remove all attachments from the mind.

Meditation should be **constant** and **uninterrupted.** To be constant and uninterrupted, it must be of the very nature of Knowledge. It cannot be a thought form, for no mental form is constant. That which is of the nature of deep, innermost Knowledge, at the very depth at which you exist, is constant. That is the true place of meditation. **In the heart,** in your quintessential Being, there should be the meditation that consists of pure Knowledge, **Consciousness, which is devoid of all adjuncts, that Siva, I am.**

Meditation truly is to identify yourself, the very essence of your Being, with pure Consciousness and not with any adjunct. By "adjunct" is meant any limiting definition, such as Consciousness plus "I," Consciousness plus the mind, Consciousness plus the senses, Consciousness plus the body, and Consciousness plus objects of perception. You should realize your nature, free of any adjunct, identifying yourself with pure Consciousness. Consciousness, realized free of any limitation whatsoever, with nothing added to it, is the real nature of Siva, and Siva is what, indeed, you are.

That you exist is true. That you exist as this thing or that thing is not true. That you are Consciousness is the truth. That you are defined by what you are aware of is not true.

Remove all attachments from the mind. In delusion, which is mere imagination, to connect the Existence of the Consciousness, which is the Self, with anything is attachment. The instruction is to remove all the attachments from the mind. If attachments are removed from the mind, what remains of the mind?

You become attached in your mind only, for there is no other place for attachment to occur. You become attached when you already consider your nature to be one of the limiting adjuncts. With that illusory appearance, you become attached, thinking "Reality is here," "I am here," "My happiness is here." The result of such attachment is just the opposite: unhappiness, illusion, and not knowing your own Self. So, remove all the attachments of the mind. The sense of reality, of identity, and of happiness return to their origin. Their origin is you. What are you? You are that which is proclaimed to be Siva, the highest absolute good, the auspicious. It is the inconceivable, illimitable Consciousness. Siva is without limitation. You should identify yourself with the unlimited Siva. This leaves no room to identify as a thinker or as one defined by his thoughts. Attachments can be removed because they are not real. If they had a speck of reality in them, they would not be removed at any time.

Attachment is the idea that the non-self is the Self. By discriminating clearly what is the Self and what is not, attachment is destroyed. Then, what remains? Just your real identity, Siva, pure Consciousness. You are not an attached individual. One suffers due to attachment. Recognizing this, one wants to be free of it. The intention is noble, virtuous, and right. The way to be completely free of the attachment is to discern your real nature, which nothing has touched, at any time.

If you identify yourself as pure Consciousness, ignorance will not be conjured up. Ignorance not being produced, there is nothing out of which to make the attachment.

Only meditation that consists of true Knowledge can be uninterrupted. Thoughts are easily interrupted. Knowledge can be continuous. Where is Knowledge? **In the heart,** the innermost recess of your existence. What should be the meditation? Not these words, but the meaning indicated by them, which is **Consciousness, devoid of all adjuncts, that Siva, I am.**

By interior knowledge you know that you exist. By such interior knowledge, divest your sense of identity of all the limiting adjuncts. They are added only in delusion, for Siva, the real Self, is innately limitless. By interior knowledge, dissolve such ignorant imagination. What are the adjuncts? They are any form the "I" takes, as a mind, as a person, as a body, as a sensing entity, and such. By this knowledge, all attachments from the mind are removed. What, then, remains of your mind? It is Brahman, Consciousness and Siva. It is to be known vividly, experientially and permanently, within you, as you. You are not the limited being. You are Being, without limitation. Where Being stands self-revealed, bliss shines fully.

The meditation is described as, **"That Consciousness, which is devoid of all adjuncts, that Siva, I am."** To be devoid of all adjuncts is to be formless, without limitation, without qualities, and without attributes. It is Consciousness as it is, not falsely connected with a body, a mind, the senses, and such. Siva is the infinite Consciousness and **I am** indicates identity. **Constant, uninterrupted meditation.** Since thought is inconstant, the meditation indicated cannot be with thought. The thought "that Consciousness which is devoid of all adjuncts, that Siva I am" is not what is indicated. The meaning expressed in those words is the thought-transcendent Reality. Meditation ought to be constant. To be constant it must be beyond the mental level. Beyond the level of the mind, there is only Consciousness, which is Knowledge. The true substance of meditation is Knowledge. Pursue meditation as Self-Knowledge, the illumination of Consciousness by Consciousness. Such is not thinking but meditation. By such meditation, all attachments from the mind are removed. When is there attachment? When

62

you think this thing or that thing is your happiness. When is there attachment? When you think this thing or that thing is real, for, obviously, if you knew it is unreal, you would not seek for happiness in it. When is there attachment? When you falsely associate your identity, your very existence, with some thought or something, which cannot be. If your mind would be bereft of all attachment, so that there is no confusion regarding identity, reality or happiness, what form would your mind have? What would remain of your mind, if your mind were completely devoid of attachment, containing no confusion whatsoever regarding yourself, what is real, and what is happiness? There would be no tendencies, no vasanas. What would remain of your mind? There would just be pure, unmixed Consciousness. Without attachment, there would be no limiting adjuncts; there would be nothing superimposed to confine. Consciousness is Siva, and Siva is your actual Existence. Thus he said, **"that Siva, I am."**

If the attachments of the mind are removed, you are quite free and happy in your natural state. How is this brought about? **Through constant, uninterrupted meditation in the heart.** The heart means your very center. Your within-ness should meditate upon its own nature. Constant, uninterrupted meditation is not possible at the level of thought. Meditation needs to be thought-transcendent to be continuous. Such thought-transcendent meditation is Self-inquiry. The meditation is expressed in these words: **That Consciousness, which is devoid of all adjuncts, that Siva, I am.** It is not that one must think that thought, but one is to inwardly realize the significance of what is stated by it. Your nature is Consciousness, without adjuncts, which means without limitations added to your nature. Setting aside limitations, the adjuncts, by inquiring, "Who am I?", meditation is the shining of the self-luminous Consciousness. The self-luminous, indestructible Consciousness, completely transcendent of thought, is Siva, and Siva alone is the significance of "I."

Verse 28

Proclaim that he who is established in Truth, through knowledge of the Self, and has destroyed the

latent impressions of the [five] sense organs through that Knowledge, is the fire of Knowledge, the possessor of the thunderbolt of Knowledge, the destroyer of time, the hero who has overcome death.

Reality is that which exists. Such is the **Truth.** Unless one knows oneself, there is not the knowledge of reality but only false appearance. If there is knowledge of yourself, you know your Existence as it is, and the Existence is the reality. It is not a part of reality, for the notion of a "part" is only when one has added some limiting adjunct to the Self, which is Existence-Consciousness. Rather, the Self is absolute Existence. The Self is the Truth. Knowledge of the Self is alone Knowledge of Reality. Reality is not a thing removed from the Self; the Self is not a particle within reality. The Self is the illimitable expanse of infinite Being-Consciousness. That is the truth. That alone is real. That alone is what you are.

To be **established in Truth** means the destruction of the **latent impressions of the sense organs through that Knowledge.** Through what knowledge? The Knowledge of Reality, the knowledge that clearly discerns that which is and that which is not. What is not? The impressions of the senses. This pertains to the entire sphere of objective experience.

The sphere of objective experience is not really external, but is merely an illusory appearance within the mind. The destruction of the world occurs in the mind. The destruction of the world in the mind is the destruction of the belief that sensations show you reality and your identity. When there is no false notion of an objective world, when there is no mistake regarding what the nature of the sensations is, Knowledge shines.

How do you go beyond the sensations? It is not by another sensation of a different kind, but by Knowledge. How do you go beyond the mind and its impressions? It is not by thinking, not by a mental mode, and not by not thinking, but by mind-transcendent Knowledge. Such is Self-Knowledge. It is Being's knowledge of itself. One who has gone beyond the world, the senses, the mind, and such is himself the **fire of Knowledge.** This is Agni portrayed in the Vedas. Then, Knowledge is no longer the means but the end itself. This is not an end removed from yourself, but rather this is your very Being. That which manifests as the means of destruction, or transcendence, is actually the reality of the Self. Knowledge is Being.

The possessor of the thunderbolt of Knowledge. Knowledge destroys ignorance in less than a moment. The one who wields the thunderbolt is none other than God, portrayed as Indra in the Vedas and Skanda in the Puranas. God is the absolute Existence-Consciousness. This is the very substance of the Knowledge.

The destroyer of time. One who has gone beyond the mind has gone beyond time, just as one who has gone beyond the body has gone beyond place. In Being, you are timeless, location-less, and not measured by anything. Being unborn, you are imperishable. The realization of yourself as That makes you the conqueror of death, mrityunjaya. How else is one to conquer death, except by realizing that one's Self is eternal Existence? No transient means will suffice to conquer death. Nothing bodily will conquer death. Of bodies, the mortality rate is one hundred percent.

That which is in the mind comes and goes in time. Only that which has no creation has no destruction. The unborn is the imperishable. Realize your own nature as unborn, and death dies. If you mistake the sensations to be real, if you have an idea of an existent world as an impression of those sensations and that you are somehow defined by such, timelessness will seem elusive and immortality a hope beyond your grasp. If you destroy the ego and its attendant notions, giving up the I-am-the-body misconception, transcending the senses, and no longer conceiving of a sphere of objective experience, immortality is your very nature. Timelessness is your very nature, with no beginning, no end, no now, no then, just one vast, self-knowing Being. That is the reality, and one who knows it is it alone. Thus, the Vedas declare, the knower of Brahman becomes Brahman.

Abidance in Truth consists of Self-Knowledge. Since the Self always is the Self, and there is only one Self, abidance cannot be an activity, a change of state, or anything pertaining to the individual, which is an illusion. Abidance is true, mind-transcendent Knowledge. To be established in Truth, know yourself, and destroy **the latent impressions of the sense organs,** through this Knowledge.

What is meant by the impressions of the sense organs? They are such ideas and tendencies that happiness may be secured externally, from any sense object, as something seen, heard, touched, tasted, or smelled. It means the tendency of considering the senses as the determination of reality, thinking that what you see, hear, touch, taste, or smell is real. How do you destroy those false impressions, or misconceptions? By the knowledge of yourself. The Self is the happiness that is sought, and it is the Self that is the Reality, and not what is sensed as the so-called world. If you leave behind such misconceptions, your knowledge of the Self will be steady, and it is by this very Knowledge that you rise above the sense impressions.

Is the fire of knowledge. From the standpoint of the individual, it seems as if knowledge is something to be obtained and possessed. Indeed, one becomes **the possessor of the thunderbolt of Knowledge,** yet the Knowledge one possesses is really the Knowledge one is. In Self-Knowledge, Being is the Knowledge, as assuredly as Being is Consciousness. It is the power of Consciousness that illumines and burns up the dross of ignorance. It is Consciousness that is all powerful. It is Consciousness that is the destroyer of time, itself being timeless. It is Consciousness that is your very Being, which is deathless, and only the deathless can be considered the conqueror of death.

In the Knowledge of the Self, the very idea of being a transmigrating jiva is lost, and that lost illusion alone is the holder of the samskaras, or latent impressions. To be beyond time, seek yourself. Seek to know yourself. To be beyond death, seek yourself. Seek to know yourself. To realize that which is glorified in countless scriptures and by countless names, seek yourself. Seek to know yourself. You are not the limited jiva. You are not the one subject to time, ignorance, death, and such. What are you? You are the Reality, Existence, which is un-sensed. Give up the idea that the senses can show you anything about reality or yourself. The Reality comprehends itself. Consciousness illumines itself. Being reposes in itself. This is the wondrous Knowledge which unfailingly liberates one from all of the imagined bondage.

Establishment in the Truth is by Knowledge alone. In true Knowledge, what you know, you are; so that one who is established in Truth is the Truth himself. He is not an embodied individual but is the Truth, infinite Being-Consciousness-Bliss, which is the real Self. **Has destroyed the latent impressions of the sense organs through that Knowledge;** what impressions? Primarily, it is the impression that the world is real. The senses do not actually create that impression, but they are the adjunct utilized by the mind, when confused, to arrive at that false impression. What do you know of the world, except what is of the senses? One who is established in the Self, as the Self, does not regard the senses as determining reality. The Reality, actual Existence, is un-sensed. If one abides firmly established in the Knowledge of the Self, by the Knowledge of the Self, and has no false notion considering the world, this one is himself **the fire of Knowledge,** which illuminates and burns up the dross of ignorance. This one is **the possessor of the thunderbolt,** depicted as Skanda, who holds the thunderbolt in his left hand. This is the Knowledge that destroys all illusion at once. This one is **the destroyer of time.** Time does not measure him; he destroys time. Similarly, such a one is **the hero who has overcome death.** He does not die; death dies. Such a one is Siva himself, the conqueror of death and the destroyer of time.

Self-Realization is not a particular sensory state. The senses are not real, and they do not determine what is real. They appear only in the waking state of mind. They do not tell you what is real, any more than your dream senses tell you what is real regarding the dream world.

The mind and prana cannot be the Reality. Without the mind and prana, can there be activity of the senses? The senses are not eternal, and they are not the Self. They are not real, and they do not determine what is real. Cease to regard yourself as a sensing entity or as anything sensed. Breath is just an animating factor for the body. It is not you.

Establishment in Truth is by Knowledge of the Self. **The Knowledge of the Self** is the Knowledge of Reality. The Self is the Reality; it is without a second. By such Self-Knowledge, the concepts and the tendencies of the mind are destroyed.

Destroyed are the belief in "I" and the belief in "this." The notion of an objectified sphere of experience, also, is destroyed. Everything that is perceived through the sense organs is no longer regarded as real. Self-Knowledge is not a relation between a subject and an object. This Knowledge is Being. The thunderbolt is associated, in the Vedas, with Indra and later, in the Puranas, with Skanda. Skanda is the hero, who, with the weapon of Knowledge, splits to pieces the delusion, which saves living beings from the dreamlike ignorance. **The destroyer of time.** How do you destroy time? The nonobjective and inconceivable is timeless, and abidance as that is the destruction of time. Time depends on two or more thoughts in order to appear. That which is entirely beyond thought is timeless. It is the ever-existent Consciousness, your true Self. Being timeless, it is without creation and destruction. It is birthless and deathless.

Verse 31

To one who is sleeping in a cart, the movement of the cart, its stopping, and its being left alone are the same. [Similarly], to the true sage who is asleep inside the gross body, activity, contemplation, and sleep [are the same].

If you regard yourself as the mind, there seem to be changes of state for you. If, inquiring, you find that you are not the mind, but the constant Consciousness, you remain unaffected by the various changes of states of the mind—waking, sleeping, meditation, and all such states, just as a traveler asleep inside a cart experiences no change, and the movement of the cart does not affect him. One who abides as pure Consciousness experiences no change of state of mind, regardless of the outer appearances of sleeping, waking, meditating, or any other change. One should know himself as the constant, immovable Consciousness and not misidentify as the mind that changes states, as an experiencer within that mind, and as if he were defined by the content of those states.

The ego neither exists nor does it have any knowing capacity. It is an imaginary person. It does not know anything. All knowledge lies in pure Consciousness, which is the ever-same Existence. You project your Existence onto that illusion and your Consciousness onto that inert illusion, but such projection is not at all real. It does not change the facts. The ego is missing; hence, Sri Ramana's analogy of the uninvited wedding guest. Indeed, all bondage is mere imagination. Liberation is freedom from such imagination. This freedom comes only by Knowledge. The ego does not exist as such, and he is himself the burden for himself. You do not liberate the individual; rather you become liberated from the idea that there is an individual. Siva is always himself.

The mind is capable of a variety of states. To consider yourself to be an appearance within those states is limited delusion. To know that the Self, space-like, is beyond the states is wisdom. To be free of identification with anything that occurs or appears in any state of mind is true Knowledge. For a man sleeping inside a cart, there is no difference whether the cart is left alone, moving, hitched up or not.

There is no difference in your Existence at any time. If you suppose that you undergo a change of state, what are you taking yourself to be? **Activity, contemplation,** or samadhi, **and sleep [are the same].** How can it be so? They are not the same for the body, but you are not the body. They obviously are not the same for the mind, for they are changes of the mind being described, but you are not the mind. For one who knows that he is not the body, but bodiless Being, changes of the body are of no consequence, and do not represent different states to him. Similarly, for one who knows that he is not the mind, but the all-transcendent Consciousness and abides as such, states of mind—waking, dreaming, sleeping, samadhi—are of no consequence. They represent no change in his state, because his state is his Existence. To attain this state, find out what, in truth, you are. You are neither active nor inactive, neither in samadhi nor out of samadhi. You are neither with a body nor without a body. You are neither with thought nor without thought. Being alone is just as it is, always. Changes to the cart do not affect the man who is asleep. Similarly, changes to the body and mind do not affect the Self. If you know yourself in this manner, you will always be at peace.

Self-Realization is only loosely spoken of as a state. It is not really a state at all, but the very nature of Existence. States or conditions are for the body, the senses, the mind and such. The Self is pure Being. Being does not have a state. It just is. States of all kinds come and go. Being remains as it is always, without appearing or disappearing. States are always something known. You are never the known. So, while, at first, one seeks to attain the supreme state, in the course of inquiry, he finds that what he is seeking is not a state to be attained, but he is seeking himself. For that, making your vision nonobjective, deeply inquire as to who you are.

If the body is like a pot, you can be said to be like the space that appears inside it. Really, space is not cooped up inside the pot. There is space inside the pot and outside the pot, and it is only one space. When the pot is formed, space does not become trapped inside it, though there seems to be space in the pot. When the pot is shattered and the space seems to rejoin the greater space, no such rejoining has actually occurred. It was always one space, in the pot, out of the pot, and pervading the pot.

Similar is it with the Self, of the nature of pure Being-Consciousness, and the inert body. If you understand yourself to be of the nature of the space of Being-Consciousness, the idea of location in relation to this pot-like body seems absurd. The senses appear to apprehend objects. More deeply understood, the senses and their objects are but figments of imagination within the waking state, apparently solidified by lending them your own reality. The senses show objects; they never show yourself. The senses, also, are a kind of object. You know about them. That which knows about them cannot be them. Right now, you have seeing, hearing, touching, etc., in various degrees, according to the operations of the sense organs and the mental attention given to them, so that one or the other predominates at any one time. Listening is predominating now, along with seeing, while tasting is not very active. At lunchtime, it will be different. These senses appear and disappear. If the senses were removed, all at once or one at a time, so that there would be no seeing, no hearing, no feeling or touching, etc., would there be any change in your existence? The manifestation of the senses or their absence makes no change in your Being. That which knows the presence or absence of the senses is beyond the senses. Being-Consciousness is not sensed and is not the senses. It is not a sensing entity. If the Self were a sensing entity, it would always have the characteristics of the senses, for whatever is the Self is always such. If it comes and goes, rises and falls, it cannot actually be the Self.

Realization and blissful immortality cannot be the results of an objective analysis. When it comes time for the body to fade away, you will want your understanding to be very experiential, won't you? Have it be that way even now and enjoy the bliss of it.

Inquiry does not aim at a change of sensory experience but a destruction of the mind. The senses are actually only an appearance in the mind. Because they are an appearance in the mind, if you merely physically seclude yourself from the sensations, the mind can continue, as vividly as before. Sensation is an appearance in the mind and an activity of the mind.

There is, in truth, no outside world sensed and no actual senses. Just as in a dream, one senses things. If, in a dream, you sense something, the thing is not actually there, and the sensation is not actually occurring. It is all in the mind, or maya. The root of the mind is the supposition of "I," who takes the form of the experiencer, of the mind, of the senses, of the body, and of the objects. By inquiring into one's nature, the individuality of him, being unreal, vanishes, along with every definition of him as an experiencer, a thinker, a sensor, etc. What remains is that which is actually present the entire time and which alone is there: the vast expanse of Being-Consciousness-Bliss. As Being, it is the only existence, without inner or outer. As Consciousness, it is the un-sensed knower of all that is sensed, the unknown knower of all that is thought. As Bliss, it shines when you know it clearly as it is. Therefore, in meditation, do not attempt so much to avoid the senses or to stop the senses, but seek the knowledge of the Self, which is already free and beyond the senses. No sensation ever touches you.

Why are such the same for the sage? It is because he knows that he is not the body. He has found his true Being, which is unaffected by the states of the body, unaffected by the states of the senses, and similarly transcendent of the states of mind.

Verse 32

Beyond the reach of those who experience the waking, dream, and sleep states, there is a state of waking-sleep, known as turiya (the fourth). As that state alone is real and as the [other] three that appear are unreal, know that turiya itself is turiyatita (beyond turiya, beyond the fourth).

Beyond the reach of those who experience the waking, dream, and sleep states. The waking person does not reach beyond the waking state, just as the dreamer does not reach beyond the dream. So it is with the sleeper. The nature of the Self is not to wake, dream or sleep. The ever-present Consciousness is not a waking one, dreamer or sleeper. Misidentification with any of the content of those states is limiting delusion. The misidentification as the experiencer of those states, whether waking, dreaming or sleeping, is also erroneous. Consciousness does not wake, dream, or sleep. It just shines continuously, free of all adjuncts, such as an experiencer of a waking state, an experiencer of a dream, and an experiencer of deep sleep. Perceive Consciousness as it is and not as endowed with limiting adjuncts.

In relation to the three states, it is named "the fourth" to indicate it is something entirely transcendent of the three states. Consciousness alone is real, and the three states, their content, and supposed experiencers are entirely unreal. They do not exist as such. What exists is the one, illimitable Consciousness, which is neither a subject nor an object. To further indicate its transcendent nature, it is also referred to as "beyond the fourth," for there is nothing else other than it for it to transcend.

Do you think you are experiencing a state of mind now? Do you consider yourself the waking experiencer? Do you regard the experiences of the waking state as the reality? If you regard yourself as the "I" that is experiencing such and assume those objects of experience to be real, the truth will seem to be beyond your grasp, even though it exists as your very Being.

Turn inward, transcending all of the states of mind. Turn inward, questioning the very nature of "I." Constant Existence cannot be a waking one, a dreamer, or a sleeper, for if your existence or consciousness were that, you would always be endowed with such states, whether waking, dreaming, or deep sleep. If the waking one were real, you would always be awake, but that is not so. If the dreamer were real, the dreams would go on forever, but such is not so. The same is the case with the deep sleep. You exist forever. What is this "you"? It is called "the fourth" in the scriptures, yet it is the original, real state, the only real state that there is. Indeed, it is not a state, but of the nature of Consciousness.

Know Consciousness free of all mental modes and free of all mental states. By modes is meant the patterns of thought within the states, whether considered to be thoughts, feelings, sensations, or the things perceived. All of them are just modes. The modes are within and according to the state in which they appear, but the Consciousness that you are lies beyond those states, vast and timeless, and not destroyed when the states disappear. Know yourself in this way.

The waking state experiencer experiences the waking state. The dreamer experiences the dream. The sleeper experiences the absence of everything else in sleep. None of these states are yours, and you are none of the three experiencers of these. Your nature is the continuous Existence that does not wake when waking occurs, does not dream when dreaming occurs, and does not sleep when sleeping occurs. To the experiencer of each state, the state seems to make sense. The very same seems as nonsense when viewed from another state. The states do not agree with each other. Dreaming and waking and sleep contradict each other. The apparent experiencer, or character within it, has contradictory knowledge from one state to another. That cannot be you.

The Reality, one's true state, the transcendent state, is beyond the three, waking, dream, and sleep, with their presence and absence of objects. This fourth state, this supreme state, is not actually a state at all, but the very nature of Consciousness. Consciousness, therefore, is declared to be "beyond the fourth." Existence is stateless. Inquire to see that you are not within a state and that you are not the experiencer of a state. You are pure Existence, steady, full, and eternal.

Beyond the reach of those who experience the waking, dream, and sleep states. As explained by Gaudapada in his *Karika* on the Mandukya Upanishad, the waking state experiencer experiences the waking state, the dreamer experiences a dream, and the deep sleeper experiences the sleep state. Considering all these as different experiencers of different states, beyond such experiencers and beyond such states is your Existence. The waking state experiencer does not reach the Existence; it is beyond his reach. Likewise is it for dream and sleep. You are not in the states of waking, dream, and sleep, and you are not the experiencer, or experiencers, of those states. What you are is the fourth, which is beyond the three states of waking, dream, and deep sleep. As the three states are not at all real, and since the fourth state is actually not a state at all but your Being, it is also **beyond the fourth.** In striving for Self-Realization, look to that which is not contained in the three states. Searching for Self-Realization, find that which is unmoved and unchanged by the three states. Though it is sought as the state of Self-Realization, when you find it, it will prove to be not a state at all but the very nature of your Being. This is transcendent of all.

The three states of waking, dream, and deep sleep, replace each other, one after another. Something remains unmoving. What is that? In waking and dreaming, there seems to be something; in deep, dreamless sleep, there seems to be nothing. The Self always exists. Consciousness is ever-existent. Described as **"the fourth,"** regarded as another state, in the context of waking, dream, and deep sleep, it is really not a state at all. The waking, dream, and sleep states are unreal. That for which you search to realize is not a state but pure Consciousness. The deep sleeper does not realize the Truth. The dreamer does not realize the Truth. The waking state character does not realize the Truth. The Truth realizes the Truth. The Truth is the infinite, nonobjective Consciousness that you truly are.

Some ask which comes first, jnana or bhakti. How can there be a first or a second when they are the same?

What is jnana, and what is bhakti? Is jnana the words and explanations associated with it or something transcending that? Is bhakti the forms, the murtis, the photographs, the singing, etc. that accompany it, or is bhakti something else? Really, bhakti is something other than the forms in which it appears; likewise is jnana. They are both of a formless nature, and, of something that is formless, there cannot be a division. We know the distinction between two things by the form of each thing, such as this hand has one form and this hand has another form. If we see it in terms of the whole body, the hands are no longer different. Likewise is it with jnana, knowledge, and bhakti, devotion. In essence, they are the same, so we cannot say which is first or which is second.

You must see jnana beyond the form in which it appears. You must likewise see bhakti, beyond the form in which it appears. If you see only the appearances, there will be all kinds of mind-numbing questions. If you see the substance, there is no division whatsoever. The actual experience that is the result of bhakti and that is the result of jnana is one and the same. Bhakti is that in which all differentiation is lost. Jnana is the same.

They are comparable to the space of the doorway. The doorway in the satsang hall is just space. The doors, the moldings, and such merely frame the space. If there were another doorway next to it, the framing would be different, but the space would be one and the same space, for there is no distinction as inside space, outside space, left space, right space, and such. Space is undivided. They are the same space, with different decorations on the doorway.

Verse 33

If one says that the sage is free from the accumulated karma from past actions (sanchita karma) and the karma now being made (agami karma), but is subject to the karma that is to be worked out in this life (prarabdha karma), that is only to satisfy others who ask about it. Know that, just as none of a man's wives can remain un-widowed on his death, so, when the doer is gone, none of the three forms of karma can survive.

It is axiomatic that Liberation is freedom from karma. Yet there may be some doubt, for which this explanation is provided, regarding what happens after liberation. After Realization of the Self, what happens to one's life, what is the rest of the story of this life? The entire story is undone. If a man with three wives dies, all of them are widows and not just two of them. Likewise, when the doer disappears, when the idea of an "I" that has karma disappears, all kinds of karma, and even the idea of one's life, are entirely dissolved. As long as the I-am-the-body misconception remains intact, this will be difficult to understand. If you cease to view in terms of the body, the ideas of karma, destiny, etc., are consumed. If you are born, you have a lifetime and a death at the end and a need for an explanation as to what causes the sequence of events of this lifetime. If you are the unborn Consciousness, or pure Brahman, do you have a lifetime? The "I" for whom such karma or destined events would apply should be inquired into.

It is prarabdha karma that appears to play out as one's destiny in this life. How can we speak of such, for one who has realized the unreality of the world and the Self's bodiless nature? Can bodiless Being be a doer? If bodiless Being is not a doer, can it be the recipient of the fruits of action?

Now, it appears that there is this lifetime and the play of karma as described. Are you in this lifetime? Where are you truly? Do you actually ever do anything? Are you an entity propelled by karma through karma? Are you not the infinite, eternal Consciousness, which does nothing and to which nothing is done by anything?

Clarity regarding one's nature is freedom from all kinds of karma. Clarity regarding one's nature implies the death of the ego and hence the analogy about the three widows. Death of the ego comes about by inquiring to know oneself. You do nothing, and nothing happens to you. In truth, you are the formless, the changeless, and the perpetually silent.

To find this karma-less state, inquire, "Who am I?" Rise entirely above defining yourself in terms of a body that could be the performer of action or the reaper of the fruits of action. For whom is prarabdha karma manifesting as destiny? Can it be for the real Self? What else is the identity of the realized, except the Self? For purposes of explanation in the course of spiritual instruction, it is sometimes said that prarabdha remains, in order to describe to the onlooker the reason for the experiences and the activities of the body of a Self-realized sage. How does the sage himself see it? He is bodiless. He is not undergoing anything. He is not involved in doing or what has been done or what has not been done. He is simply Being, immortal Being, motionless Being. If the misidentification with the body is thoroughly abandoned, what is indicated in this verse becomes self-evident.

Verse 35

What is the use of learning, for those who do not seek the source of their birth and attempt to erase the writ of fate? They are like a gramophone. Tell me, O Lord of Sonagiri (Arunachala), what else are they?

What is the use of spiritual learning, unless you apply what you learn? The proper application is to **seek the source of their birth,** which is from where the sense of identity, or "I," springs. Without knowledge of your existence, what have you really learned? If there is knowledge of your Existence, born of deep inquiry to determine what it is, you have truly learned. Then, you understand. Merely to repeat, in the mind or verbally, statements regarding the truth, without it being experiential and conclusive within you, is like being a **gramophone.** It would just be repetition or replication of the sound without the significance. One should not be like that, but should have the bliss, the sheer joy, of experientially verifying within the significance of what he learns. It is the experiential verification within that is the actual dawning of Knowledge.

From where was the "I" born? The reference is not to the body. It is the sense of "I." From where does the sense of "I" spring? Seek the source of that birth, and realize the unborn, eternal Truth.

Familiarity with the words is not an end in itself. If one makes that an end in itself, conceiving ideas for each of the words, within the context of non-inquiry, he is **like a gramo-**

phone, merely repeating sounds and not understanding truly what they indicate.

It is necessary to actually seek the source of "I," and, thereby, find the reality of the Self. It is from the reality of the Self that the original utterances that we find in the scriptures were made. If you are inquiring, they will always be new for you, sparkling fresh, with the Truth that shines through them. If you merely learn to speak with nondual verbiage but not actually experience the bliss of true Knowledge, it is ridiculous.

Seek your source experientially. In this way, the teachings come alive for you, and they dwell within you. You come to abide at the very source of the spiritual instruction, and you dwell in the state from which it was originally uttered.

What is the use of learning about spiritual matters, unless you actually inquire, seeking your origin, the **source of your birth,** the source from which the "I" springs? It is pointless. From your spiritual learning, you should be inspired to dive within and actually inquire, in order to release yourself from the illusion of all the bondage. Apply what you learn in spiritual practice so that you never suffer again. The application in practice is the one-pointed inquiry to find out the source of "I." Who am I?

Verse 38

Who is there besides the Self? What does it matter whether one is praised or blamed? Without differentiating between oneself and others and without swerving from one's natural state, one should abide as the Self.

One's own opinions are of no consequence. Likewise are the opinions of others. There is one Self that exists and not a multiplicity of selves. You should realize the one Self by abiding as that. Abidance is knowledge. Do not swerve. Cease to misidentify. That is all that you have to do. Inquire deeply and thus cease to misidentify. Then, you will find yourself to be immovable. Praise and blame, compliments and criticism, will feel the same to you. You are beyond both. No one can adequately praise the Self, and no one can actually blame it. It is the stainless, perfect Existence.

What is there besides the Self? **Who is there besides the Self?** There is no second self in you or in anyone else. The personal entity is not real. Whether that entity is praised or blamed is equally unreal and of no significance to one who knows. Do you not first have to think of yourself as a body, and then you can think of other bodies as representing other selves? Though there may be a multiplicity of bodies, there is actually no multiplicity of selves. There is only one Self. To see how this is true, dive within and know yourself.

If you are not the body, no one else is a body. So, how do you tell the difference between yourself and someone else? If you are not the ego, or individual, others are likewise not individuals. So, can they be other? The state in which the Self remains undivided, without the least trace of differentiation, is the natural state. It is innate. It is what is true. You should abide as That. The practice of Knowledge is only to eradicate the difference born of ignorance. This accomplished, you find that the natural state is the only state. This is the state of the Self.

Praise and blame are only for the ego and are usually connected with the mind and its activities, speech and its activities, and the body and its activities. What do any of them have to do with you? Neither praise nor blame can touch the Self. They do not pertain to it. **Who is there besides the Self?** Is there an ego? Find this out by profound, steady inquiry. **Without differentiating between oneself and others,** for such differentiation is based on the "I am the body" misconception, and **without swerving from one's natural state, one should abide as the Self.** What is your natural state? It is abidance as the Self. What is natural is innate. What is innate is neither acquired nor lost. You should abide, which is to know yourself, as the innate, the natural. Do not swerve from it. Cease to misidentify with anything else. If you so abide, you realize that there is neither an individual self nor others. There is just one endless Self. This is what exists, and this is what you are. If you identify yourself in this way, if you know yourself in this way, do praise or blame mean anything to you at all?

For whom are praise and blame? If nobody is there to be the recipient of them, is there any bondage? The Self is not praised, and the Self is not blamed. If you abide as the Self, you are completely detached from praise, blame and such. It is as if someone were speaking about someone else; it does not refer to you. If you feel that you need help when you are praised or blamed, the help is stated in the verse. The help is the abidance in the Self. If we abide in the Self, we are no longer in need of help, and we remain ever thankful for the divine help of Sri Bhagavan.

What are you? You are not a thing, yet not nothing. To be as you are is not an activity; it is not a doing. To be as you are, inquire, "Who am I?"

Verse 39

Retain at heart always the sense of nonduality, but never express it in action. My son, the sense of nonduality may apply to the three worlds, but it is not to be used towards the guru.

Always retain **the sense of nonduality** in your heart. Be constantly abiding in the devoted Knowledge. **Never express it in action.** What action is a nondual action? Nonduality transcends the very idea of an actor and his action. To be devoid of such concepts is nondual. To think that there is a nondual way of acting is to miss the point utterly. **The sense of nonduality may apply to the three worlds,** which are the entire scope of all that is experienced, the entire universe and beyond, for such is the nondual Existence. **But it is not to be used towards the guru.** Sri Ramana said this, and Sri Sankara said this. Why is this advice given? Why is nonduality not to be applied to the guru? The wise saints and sages have brought forth this instruction and have themselves applied it. You can see the nondual truth in all, everywhere, but never use it in relation to the guru. This is something to contemplate.

Nonduality ought to be realized deep within. What nonduality signifies is the unalterable, invariable, absolutely singular nature of the Self. Retain the knowledge of that in your heart. However, never attempt to **express it in action.** What would be a nondual action? The very idea of such is absurd. Much of the spiritual instruction concerning nonduality involves sweeping negations. What is negated is the ignorance. This should not be thought of as some peculiar set of actions. There is no such thing as a nondual action. Nonduality signifies freedom from definition in terms of all action. Detachment, discrimination, and such are all elevated far above the plane of action. Retain the spirit of nonduality deep in your heart. There the Truth is realized. Let your actions be a manifestation of what is satyam, sivam, sundaram—the true, the good, and the beautiful.

One who truly knows remains ever-devoted. Having come upon such Knowledge, how could one not be devoted? **The sense of nonduality may apply to the three worlds,** that which is gross, that which is subtle, and that which is causal, the entirety of what is experienced, but the sadguru is beyond the three worlds and is utterly transcendent. One who lacks in constant, sustained, continuing devotion does not really know the Knowledge. The sadguru ever remains the sadguru. In books composed by Adi Sankaracarya, the pinnacle of expression of nonduality, in which he declares that there is no guru and no disciple, he concludes with, "This was composed by Sankara, who is the disciple of the glorious Guru, Govinda." There is certainly no contradiction in it. When Nidagha is enlightened by Ribhu and sees beyond all duality, he praises his guru. Asked to explain his own experience, he describes it, in sweeping, nondual terms, including statements that there is no guru and no disciple, and then he gives praise to the guru.

If you understand the secret of this, your abode is profound happiness. If devotion and knowledge are inextricable, there is real devotion, and there is real Knowledge. If they are separated in one's experience, to any degree, then, while one may be on the path, he has yet to arrive.

The instruction is threefold in this verse. The first is one should **retain at heart always the sense of nonduality.** Nonduality is interior Knowledge. One should not deviate from this Knowledge, ever. To deviate, through imagination only, from the Knowledge of the nondual, is to make yourself capable of suffering. It is to create the samsara. To abide in the nondual Knowledge, in which the Self is Brahman, is perfect peace and complete happiness. All of this is interior; it is something to be known within you. That is the first point of the verse.

The second point is **but never express it in action.** Nonduality is of the nature of Knowledge. There is no particular action that is nondual. Indeed, such does not make any sense at all. This is precious advice for the spiritual aspirant who seeks the highest Truth. Such a seeker recognizes that which is holy and important, adheres to it, embraces it, sustains it, and does not deviate from it. Such a seeker most certainly does not try to strike a balance between the samsara, or the worldly, and the spiritual and the liberating, thinking that such a deluded mixture is nondual. To mix together illusion and the truth is not nondual. Nonduality is a state of interior Knowledge. There is no action that is nondual. Action pertains to the body. The nondual Knowledge is transcendent of the body. Nondual Knowledge destroys the objective world. To try to express that in action would be absurd.

The third point is **the sense of nonduality may apply to the three worlds,** which are the gross, the subtle, and the causal, meaning universally applicable, **but it is not to be used towards the guru.** Nonduality is the Truth, yet devotion remains. In nonduality, the Self is known to be identical with the Supreme. Nevertheless, although we may say, "Om Namo Bhagavate Sri Ramanaya," we do not insert our own names into the holy mantra. Why? The reason should be self-evident, and the humility quite natural and consistent. The aspirant should not waste his precious time with the guru, by simply repeating aloud the words of instruction that he has received, saying "I am the Self, I am Brahman," etc. The guru already knows that, so the communication does not serve any purpose. Rather, the spiritual aspirant should use the precious time with the guru wisely, devotedly, and humbly. The purpose of the sacred association with the guru is the eradication of the illusion born of an ego and thereby to experientially, interiorly, in the heart, retain and realize the nondual Knowledge.

Sri Bhagavan has explained that that which is known as God appears as the guru to reveal the Self to the disciple. Thus, the three, God, Guru and the Self, are One and the same. You should not, though, attribute the oneness to the ego, not even a trace of it. In Realization, the guru is never negated; one's so-called self is negated. The guru never disappears; the disciple disappears.

If one wants the guru to no longer be a guru, such a person never had a guru, and such a person does not understand what a guru is. The objective aspect of one's experience falls away. The individuality of the disciple falls away. The disciple disappears. The guru, who is the absolute Self without the least trace of difference, remains. Who could help but love that? One who would say that he does not need a guru would be better off, according to the Maharshi's instruction, worshiping God until ripe; then, God appears in the form of a guru to reveal the Self.

If one takes the approach of giving all to the guru, all sense of "my" is lost. Where "my" is lost, "I" also subsides. The absence of "I" and "my" characterize Liberation. The guru is the guarantee of Liberation, as assured as one's own existence is. One may have a doubt about one's nature, but the guru has no such doubt. He is certainty itself, Knowledge itself. He stands as immovable Being. All the disciple or devotee can do is dissolve in him and be lost in bliss.

Verse 40

I will proclaim truly the essence of the conclusion arrived at by all the Vedantic texts. It is, that, if the ego dies and the "I" becomes That, Brahman, that "I," which is of the form of Consciousness, alone remains.

The death of the ego is by the realization of its unreality, by cessation of misidentification, and by steady inquiry to know what, in truth, you are. **If the ego dies and the "I" becomes That,** with the cessation of misidentification as an ego, That, Brahman, is realized fully to be the nature of "I." There is no other kind of "I." **That "I," which is of the form of Consciousness,** the nature of Consciousness. What form does the "I" have? Just Consciousness. **That "I,"** Consciousness, **alone remains.** No ego or anything else remains. Just Consciousness remains. Therefore, make every effort to bring about the extinction of the ego, so that your sense of identity is solely That, Brahman, One without a second. The effort is best applied in the steady inquiry, "Who am I?"

There is, then, no world, no ego, no bondage, no striving, no sadhana to be practiced, no separate state of liberation, no birth, and no death. There is just one everlasting Consciousness, the true Being of "I." Practice ardently to dissolve the illusory ego, for, in the dissolution of the ego, you know the Self, and what you know is what you are.

Five Verses on the One Self

1. He who is forgetful of the Self, mistaking the physical body for it, and goes through innumerable births, is like one who wanders all over the world in a dream. Thus, realizing the Self would only be like waking up from the dream wanderings.

Inquire into that which has been overlooked. It is your own Self, the immediate Existence. There is nothing between you and it. It is as if one had just overlooked himself. When you overlook your fundamental Being, you may mistake yourself to be a body and to be wandering through innumerable births, dream upon dream, bubbles of illusion within bubbles of illusion. Knowledge puts an end to the illusion. True knowledge is to wake up from such dream wanderings. Wandering in this world, wandering in another world, in this life, in another life, how long has such wandering gone on? No one can say. When you wake up, you know that it never occurred, and the timeless Reality is known.

2. One who asks himself "Who am I? and where am I?" though existing all the while as the Self, is like a drunken man who inquires about his own identity and whereabouts.

Who is it that asks himself "Who am I"? How can one not know the Self? Who is it that inquires? Where do you assume yourself to be? What are you taking yourself to be? Existing all the while as the Self, you are the Self, so who is ignorant of what? Who does not know whom?

3. While in fact the body is in the Self, he who thinks that the Self is within the insentient body is like one who considers the cloth of the screen, which supports a cinema picture, to be contained within the picture.

85

The body appears only in the Self. The Self does not appear in the body. You are not the body, and you are not in the body. The body offers you no definition whatsoever.

4. Does an ornament exist apart from the gold of which it is made? Where is the body apart from the Self? He who considers the body to be himself is an ignorant man. He who regards himself as the Self is the enlightened one, who has realized the Self.

Gold is not an ornament, but the ornament is nothing but gold. Whatever shape the ornament may assume and however different the ornaments are, there is only one reality, namely gold. So also [is it] with the bodies and the Self. The single reality is the Self. (Talks with Sri Ramana Maharshi 396 April 12, 1937)

The body is not the Self, but the body and anything else are not apart from the Self. There is no other existence but the one Existence. The name and the form, the perceived and the conceived, do not exist apart from the nameless and the formless. There are not two conditions, with name and without, with form and without, etc., but rather there is just one Existence, whether called "the universe," "the body," or anything else. There is just this one Existence, and the Existence ought to be known as it is. It is entirely undifferentiated.

Does an ornament exist apart from the gold of which it is made? There is gold in the ring. There is no ring apart from the gold. Gold is the only substance. The ring is just a name given. Gold is the only substance there. Likewise, the Self, of the nature of sat-chit-ananda, is the only Existence. Whether seen or unseen, it alone is. When you think that you see something else, experience something else, know something else, it is still only that considered in such a form. The substance in itself, the gold in the analogy, is utterly formless. What form does gold have? The substance itself is formless. You are that substance, the Reality.

To define yourself in terms of the body constitutes ignorance. To regard yourself as the Self is Enlightenment. Such is Realization of the Self. Therefore, give your full focus to what you consider to be your identity. What is it that is truly your existence?

Realizing your freedom from the body is very important. If you can just discern clearly, with certainty, that you are not the body, everything else will fall into place. The realization that you are not the body also means freedom from the activities, conditions, attributes, etc., of the body. If you are not the body, who are you, where are you? So important is this that three of the five verses in this text (verses 1, 3 and 4) focus exclusively on freedom from the body.

You are the Self; always only the Self. Liberate yourself from the misidentification with the body, and find that which you always are. How can one express this Knowledge, the reality of true Being?

5. The one Self, the sole Reality, alone exists eternally. When even the ancient teacher, (Adi Guru), Dakshinamurti, revealed it through speechless eloquence, who else could convey it by speech?

In the temple of Being
The space of Consciousness
Om Sri Ramanarpanamastu
Om May this be an offering to Sri Ramana

Made in the USA
Columbia, SC
28 September 2020